Make Room fo

Recent Titles in
Libraries Unlimited Professional Guides for Young Adult Librarians
C. Allen Nichols and Mary Anne Nichols, Series Editors

Extreme Teens: Library Services to Nontraditional Young Adults
Sheila B. Anderson

A Passion for Print: Promoting Reading and Books to Teens
Kristine Mahood

The Teen-Centered Book Club: Readers into Leaders
Bonnie Kunzel and Constance Hardesty

Teen Programs with Punch: A Month-by-Month Guide
Valerie A. Ott

Serving Young Teens and 'Tweens
Sheila B. Anderson, editor

The Guy-Friendly Teen Library: Serving Male Teens
Rollie Welch

Serving Urban Teens
Paula Brehm-Heeger

The Teen-Centered Writing Club: Bringing Teens and Words Together
Constance Hardesty

More Than MySpace: Teens, Librarians, and Social Networking
Robyn Lupa, Editor

Visual Media for Teens: Creating and Using a Teen-Centered Film Collection
Jane Halsall and R. William Edminster

Teen-Centered Library Service: Putting Youth Participation into Practice
Diane P. Tuccillo

Booktalking with Teens
Kristine Mahood

MAKE ROOM FOR TEENS!

Reflections on Developing Teen Spaces in Libraries

Michael Garrett Farrelly

Libraries Unlimited Professional Guides for Young
Adult Librarians Series
C. Allen Nichols and Mary Anne Nichols, Series Editors

LIBRARIES UNLIMITED

AN IMPRINT OF ABC-CLIO, LLC
Santa Barbara, California • Denver, Colorado • Oxford, England

Library of Congress Cataloging-in-Publication Data

Farrelly, Michael Garrett.
  Make Room for Teens! : Reflections on Developing Teen Spaces in Libraries / Michael Garrett Farrelly.
      p. cm. — (Libraries Unlimited Professional Guides for Young Adult Librarians Series)
  Includes bibliographical references and index.
  ISBN 978-1-59158-566-4 (pbk. : acid-free paper)
  1. Young adults' libraries — United States.   2. Libraries and teenagers.
  3. Libraries — Space utilization.   I. Title.
    Z718.5.F38   2011
    027.62'60973—dc22   2010051620

ISBN: 978-1-59158-566-4
EISBN: 978-1-59884-910-3

15 14 13 12 11   1   2   3   4   5

This book is also available on the World Wide Web as an eBook.
Visit www.abc-clio.com for details.

Libraries Unlimited
An Imprint of ABC-CLIO, LLC

ABC-CLIO, LLC
130 Cremona Drive, P.O. Box 1911
Santa Barbara, California 93116-1911

This book is printed on acid-free paper (∞)

Manufactured in the United States of America

To Maureen Farrelly, Elise Miller, Mary Lou Miller, and April Jackson. Four women who made me a better man.

CONTENTS

SERIES FOREWORD

We firmly believe that teens should be provided equal access to library services, and that those services should be equal to those offered to other library customers. This series supports that belief. That is why we are so excited about *Make Room for Teens! Reflections on Developing Teen Spaces in Libraries*. Michael Farrelly regularly shares his thoughts on teen services in his column in *Public Libraries*. Now he focuses his writing to tackle the issue of teen space in libraries. This work will provide the inspiration to allow you to create or enhance that space to provide effective services to this critical population.

We are proud of our association with Libraries Unlimited/ABC-CLIO, which continues to prove itself as the premier publisher of books to help library staff serve teens. This series has succeeded because our authors know the needs of those library employees who work with young adults. Without exception, they have written useful and practical handbooks for library staff.

We hope you find this book, as well as our entire series, to be informative, providing you with valuable ideas as you serve teens and that this work will further inspire you to do great things to make teens welcome in your library. If you have an idea for a title that could be added to our series, or would like to submit a book proposal, please email us at lu-books@lu.com. We'd love to hear from you.

Mary Anne Nichols
C. Allen Nichols

ACKNOWLEDGMENTS

This book would not be possible without the help of Elise Miller, M.L.I.S., whose assistance as both sounding board and researcher was invaluable. I'd also like to thank the staff of the Budlong Woods branch of the Chicago Public Library for providing me with a home away from home to work on the book. Thank you to Kathleen Hughes at *Public Libraries* for her editorial support and April Jackson for proofing my work from the outline on. I would also like to thank my mother, Maureen, whose encouragement and impatience with my dithering was always an inspiration. I'd also like to thank C. Allen Nichols and Barbara Ittner for their job-like patience with this first-time author. Thank you all so very much.

INTRODUCTION: WHERE DO WE PUT THEM?

There used to be no such thing as teenagers.

The modern concept of the adolescent is just that, a modern construction, which has more to do with the rapid industrialization of the 19th century than the swinging sounds of rock and roll.

The dawning of the industrial age saw children entering the industrial workforce. While the work itself was of a new variety, the idea of children working alongside adults was hardly a new concept. Apprenticeships and family farms were a common method of learning a trade or passing on an agricultural lifestyle. The massive scale of industry and the growing concern over children's well-being (physical, mental, and in some cases moral) led to the establishment of children's welfare organizations. These earth youth advocates fought for laws protecting children from harsh conditions.

The demarcation of children as a protected class had a manifold impact on American society. The concept that older children, or young adults, would have some legal rights of adults, such as the ability to work, led to another bifurcation and the rise of youth culture.

The term *teen-ager* was first used in 1941, according to the *Oxford English Dictionary*. Soon after the end of World War II, the concept of teenagers and teen culture would become one of the most defining aspects of 20th-century America. The post–World War II baby boomers became a generation of children raised in a time of unprecedented prosperity.

These so-called boomers came to enjoy an extended childhood that previous generations, faced with the hardship of the Depression and conflicts in Europe, had been denied. As this generation matured, the dichotomy of being part-child and part-adult in the eyes of society fostered the creation of a unique youth culture.

Music played a key part in this generational divide. Teenagers flocked to the early sounds of rock and roll and quickly made it the sound of their generation. The evolution of that rock and roll over the next few decades would move from pop songs of clean-cut crooners, to the psychedelic jams of the sixties. The war in Vietnam proved a powerful flashpoint for the baby boomer generation as their involvement in and opposition to the war shaped everything from their politics to their sense of style.

The children of the boomers, Generation X, would further define the divide between child and teenager. A generation raised almost entirely on television that engaged fictional realities, such as *Star Wars,* with an undreamt of passion. Gen Xers were raised more as consumers than citizens, with a disaffection for process that had been carried over from their parents. The gloomy music of grunge spoke of a longing for something more substantive and meaningful.

Generation Y or the so-called iPod generation, a name that behooves its consumerist aesthetic, has seen an explosion in consumer technology unlike anything experienced since the industrial revolution. They have watched more television, consumed more media, and processed more data than any of their forerunners. They are interconnected with commutation technology that often baffles their parents in its complexity. It is a generation that demands more and better service and expects what previous generations believed to be luxury. The generation after them, still developing its own sobriquet, has even sharper appetites, raised on the instant satisfaction of YouTube™, and the interconnectivity of MySpace™ and Facebook™.

Throughout this century of the teenager, servicing teenagers have posed any number of questions for librarians. Whether it was the old, and blessedly defunct, model of simply keeping them quiet or keeping them out, or the infinitely more inclusive modern approach of library as communal space for patrons of all ages, teens pose tough challenges for library spaces.

How do we, as librarians, plan spaces for these hyperconnected teenagers? How do we make room for teens?

In the course of this book, we'll look at the unique challenges posed by young adults, the ways in which libraries can react to ever-present concept of *cool*, the ways in which transformative spaces work well, and techniques for creating spaces that allow teens to feel ownership. We'll look at how stereotypes about teens both bind and liberate, and talk about some best practices for designing a library space for teens.

The teenagers of the 21st century are more connected than previous generations, and they are constantly being bombarded by media with countless opportunities for entertainment and social outlets. Defining the library space as something unique and wholly distinct is the great challenge for this generation.

1

◇ ◇ ◇

UNIQUE CHALLENGES

It's usually feast or famine.

Perhaps there are days when the young adults section is so quiet a pin-dropping contest could be held. Maybe it's so empty, a brass band could march up and down the aisles blasting the finest of John Philips Sousa. A bright sunshiny day, a perfect autumn day, or a free admission day at the local water park have all stolen away young adult patrons. Curmudgeons rejoice while young adult librarians catch up on their paperwork and book ordering.

Then there are the days when it seems that word has gotten out that the library is giving away free game consoles. The flood of teens never seems to stop, tables are filled to overflowing, and tally sheets for reference questions get marked up so much someone finally writes "A LOT!" and gives up the ghost. Curmudgeons wag their fingers and young adult librarians wish for four extra arms and two extra heads to keep up.

Spaces for young adults are study spaces that will see extreme rates of use on a daily, perhaps even hourly basis. Libraries, often bastions of a far more sedate mindset and usage plan, can be challenged in keeping pace. The unique challenges of young adult patrons can seem daunting, but in reality they can be broken down into a few clear areas of focus.

OUTREACH

While patrons of any age are welcome in the library, young adults are often the subject of specific outreach efforts. School visits from librarians are one very common way of getting in touch with teens in a community. Bookmobiles, library involvement in local events, and media outreach are also fairly common. Outreach through new media, Web sites, blogs, podcasting, and social networking are also emerging as means of getting the message out to young adults about what libraries have to offer.

The challenge in outreach is finding what are truly effective lures for an audience as fickle and often media-savvy as young adults. The saturation of advertisement in the media has reached such a point that it is often difficult for adults to discern between ads and content. To stand out amidst the churn of ads, libraries have to be clear, concise, and unique in their "pitch" to the young adult audience. Fortunately libraries offer a wholly distinct range of services and opportunities; it's simply a matter of communicating that to teens.

BEHAVIOR

The assumption is that young adults are not interested in libraries. They are bored by books and are more interested in the ephemera of pop culture than in the stately bookshelves and hallowed dusty halls of their local library. When they do enter a library, teens are little more than a nuisance, best shooed out into the street with a stern hand to leave the librarians in peace amidst the moldering shelves. Such a tired and trite notion speaks ill not only of youth but of public libraries as an institution. Are libraries to be morgues of knowledge? Monuments to dead words and dead ideas? Hallowed and holy sacred spaces that are best not trod by quick and clever feet? This notion is, of course, nonsense.

Young adults can be noisy, rambunctious, discourteous, challenging, clever, and willfully ignorant of staid forms of propriety. It is then the challenge of young adult librarians to give these wild things a place to engage in their rumpus; to mold that energy along constructive lines, knowing that it is the energy of creation that filled those shelves in the first place.

PROGRAMMING

Perhaps the greatest challenge of all is what to do with young adults when they do come to the library. In recent years, public libraries have grown more and more aware of the dire need for engaging activities for children and young adults outside of the school environment. Young adults are especially in need of "something to do" as they are faced with near adult capacities while at the same time limited by their age and experience.

Casting yourself back to the age of 15 or 16, think of how many places you were not allowed to go. Concert venues, bars, night clubs, even some stores were barred to you. The police seemed like a hostile force when it came to matters of curfew and "loitering," and even schools would often try to roust students from their grounds once the final bells had rung. If you didn't have a dedicated activity (sports or clubs), you were often given an askance glance by large swaths of society. Libraries have too often taken part in that supposition that teens are just up to no good.

COLLECTION DEVELOPMENT

Teens consume culture at a rate that often boggles the minds of older people. The image of a young adult thumbing a mobile phone while on a computer and carrying on a conversation is almost passé. Teens that have grown up native to the information age are connected and interconnected in ways that their parents could have only dreamt of at that age. So how do librarians choose information resources, literature, and other materials for a group of voracious data consumers?

The young adult book market is one of the fastest growing and most diverse in all of literature. While other aspects of the publishing industry face narrowing readership, teen readers are driving a variety of genres. Beyond books, teens consume massive quantities of music, films, and video materials. A young adult might come in asking for an album from a classic 1970s punk group like Iggy and the Stooges one week and look for something from art rockers like Radiohead the next. Developing a collection that is not only vibrant but expansive is a massive challenge for young adult librarians.

WHY BOTHER? THEY'RE JUST GOING TO CHEAT

Faced with these challenges, which can easily eat into budgets, space, time, and sanity, it's easy to see why some give in to apathy.

Why bother trying to keep up with the trends in taste of literature for teens when you can just add whatever is at the top of the sales charts and has a starred review? Why develop programming that draws in new faces when it just makes a lot of noise and mess? Why try to work with young adults to develop codes of behaviors, when some of them are just going to ignore it anyway?

As a young librarian I faced this very attitude while working on a redevelopment of a young adult reading program. Another librarian said that my plan (which put more power in the hands of the teens, removed arbitrary rules and made the whole program more interactive and participatory) was flawed because "They're going to cheat anyway. They always do." I remember being at a loss for words for this argument, as it seemed to be the very antithesis of what engaged me in young adult librarianship in the first place. The assumption that teens are generally up to no good, that efforts to reach them are flawed at best and a waste of resources at worst, that it's better to simply let kids between the ages of 12 and 18 just disappear from the library rather than make an effort to engage them at their level was, to me, completely wrong.

Any patron group, from young mothers to senior citizens, from NASCAR dads to the homebound, present their own unique set of challenges. Libraries are tasked with reaching out to the whole of the community, regardless of the difficulty level in doing so. Failure is just simply not an option that any right-thinking librarian can live with.

The rewards of meeting the challenges presented by young adults are staggering. Guiding young people from story times and lap sits through crafting and macaroni art into book clubs and movie night and gaming socials onto open mic nights and poetry readings is a process that helps produce more fully involved, fully engaged members of the community as a whole.

Of course, adults who have seen the impact of libraries since they were young children are all the more likely to support libraries as institutions as well. So in meeting the unique challenges of young adults as patrons, libraries serve not only the noble interests of the community as a whole, but the more immediate interests of the library as an institution.

2
◇ ◇ ◇

LIBRARIES AND COOLNESS

THE LIBRARY IS COOL

I would be doing a disservice to my generation of library professionals if I didn't mention *Buffy the Vampire Slayer*. Besides cats, no other cultural touchstone seems to connect librarians more than kibitzing about Buffy, and more specifically her librarian mentor Rupert Giles.

For those baffled by the reference, I'll explain. Buffy, the television show not the ill-fated film, was the story of a young woman who is "chosen" to fight demons, monsters, and yes, vampires. She is a normal high school student by day and a hunter of the undead by night. For much of the series run each episode would feature Buffy engaged in a bit of research, usually trying to sleuth out the weakness of that week's vile creature. For the first few years, Buffy and her friend's high school years, this research took place in a school library. That's right, demon-hunters in a library. It was not uncommon for spells and fights and climatic moments to take place "@" the library, to paraphrase the ALA (American Library Association).

Now, unless your library is like the Sunnydale High facility, which conveniently featured a massive selection of obscure occult materials, you're unlikely to have that level of sheer coolness, even in a "Teen Zone." But this is not to say that libraries cannot be cool. But chasing coolness can be as deadly as hot-footing it through a graveyard after a bloodsucking fiend with a blunt wooden stake. This chapter will talk about coolness and how libraries can embrace some simple practices to avoid gruesome demise, and by gruesome demise, I mean a "decrease in young adult patron satisfaction."

BAD FADS

I nearly lost an eye to a fad. I was 13 years old and it was the year of the slap bracelet. These gaudy pieces of plastic, often covered in some kind of cloth material, were all the rage in my grammar school. The gimmick of the bracelets was simple: a stiff six-inch piece of plastic that curled into a cuff when struck. It appealed to young adults on a visceral level for many reasons.

First, it was a thing that became another thing. The concept of instant change is almost hypnotic at any age, but especially so at an age when most change seems either glacial (the progression towards adulthood) or nigh instant (puberty). Second, slap bracelets had a certain patina of violence to them. While many girls in my class looked to the aesthetics of the bracelets, the boys in my class were peeling the cloth layers off to expose the rough hewn plastics beneath. Slap bracelets weaponized very quickly.

I had the misfortune of turning my head too quickly while one of my classmates decided to play Oppenheimer and nearly found myself wearing a patch. While that might have made me appear quite jaunty, presaging the cultural fascination with pirates by a decade or two, I'm glad that fate had other plans.

Fads are not just dangerous to the ocular cavities of nascent librarians. They're hazardous to libraries as a whole.

A SLAVE TO FASHION

Attempting to keep up with trends in teenage culture and fashion is an industry unto itself. An excellent satire of the nonsense of predicting stuff "for kids" is the Coen Brothers marvelous film *The Hudsucker Proxy*. In the movie a not-too bright guy, played by Tim Robbins, becomes the head of a massive conglomerate somewhat by accident. His sole good idea is a circle on a piece of paper that he repeatedly shows to people crying "Y'know, for kids." He is met with a wall of blank stares until he actually creates the object and the company becomes massively successful. You see, that silly little circle that everyone derided just needed a good name: the Hula Hoop.

Untold billions are spent every year to create the next gadget or toy or plastic item to catch the fickle and omnivorous eye of the teenage market. Teens like cell phones, but will they like cell phone charms? Teens like to hang out and chat with friends, but will they like doing that at a square table or one with built-in games or one that doubles as an air-hockey table? Or forget the table entirely. Let's make a pow-wow circle with stuffed little cubes. Or maybe that pirate trend is coming back, and we should have treasure chests filled with book booty. Is that too much?

The answer is, definitively, yes.

Let's look at three kinds of "trendy" furniture and their pros, which are few, and their cons, which are legion.

INFLATABLE CHAIRS

The first time I saw one of these beasts was in college. It was plastered with beer logos and sat, half-inflated, in the corner of a dorm room. No one had the will, or energy, to fill it completely. I wondered just how much beer-breath remained trapped inside.

The pros of an inflatable chair seem obvious. They're fun, often very colorful and seem to come straight from an era of plastic fantastic enjoyment. They also seem practical on some level. No need to strain the backs of library workers rearranging furniture for en event, just give these chair a push or a toss.

The cons are just as obvious. One sharp pen or pencil jab, and you go from chair to rubber puddle all too quick. Assuming that jab is of the accidental variety. These chairs are prone to popping all on their own under enough weight or even a sudden sitting. The embarrassment of a teen being told that the fun furniture popped because they're too heavy is not something any librarian wants on their conscience.

Finally, there's simply a level of tackiness to these things, a sense of impermanence, simple goofiness that teens can pick up on as easily as adults. As if we are saying "this space for young adults is not built to last." A temporary environment is an anathema to every other space in the library, which screams permanence, security, timelessness.

BEAN BAGS

Ah, the simple and majestic bean bag; this stalwart of youth, this icon of a slackadaisical generation, like a sceptered isle of laziness awash in the mellow fruitfulness of simpler days. Keats and Shakespearean mangling aside, the bean bag chair seems to have a great deal going for it.

First off, it's simple. It's a flop space, suitable for the teenagers who simply crash down at the end of the school day. Somewhat akin to those enormous cushions they put under stuntmen. Bean bags are also shape-able. They can be piled up against the wall as a pseudo-seat or shoved in a mass to create something of a blob-like biomass.

But it's just that pliable nature that makes the bean bags such a failure in terms of form. Bean bags tend to wander. If you're trying to define a space as being for and about teens, it's made all the harder when the teen furniture goes strolling into the storybook lounge or gets stacked up for a truly epic back flip off a table.

Yes, back flip. Bean bags are all but invitations to pull all manner of mad stunts on. They give the illusion of being safe for jumping on, which they are to a very limited degree, and are just so very tempting. Your humble author will confess to more than a few attempts at gymnast-style greatness with bean bags. Thankfully the cast only covered half my leg for that summer.

"RESTAURANT STYLE" BOOTHS

To call this style of furniture out as less than perfect is sure to ruffle more than a few feathers. Booth seating has become something of a trend piece for young adult spaces over the past decade. The appeal is obvious; the drawbacks, less so.

It's simplicity itself to see the appeal of booth seating. What teenager worth their salt hasn't spent hours on end in a restaurant booth with friends just hanging out and chatting? The space feels intimate and yet communal all at once. It harkens back to a communal dining experience that most young adults simply do not experience at home.

These booths are often expensive, coming in pieces and not as a whole. For instance, a single bench seat, one half of the booth, prices out at around $600 through a large library services provider. Thus both sides of the booth are $1,200 plus another $300 for the table. A grand total of $1,500 before shipping (which could be very costly) and any assembly costs. Restaurant suppliers have comparable prices though one might get lucky with second-hand merchants. This expense might be minimal to some libraries, but to others it might eat up the whole budget.

The return on investment might not be worth it. You have seating for four, comfortably, and six, uncomfortably. Likely less than that if you add in bags and books and coats and general claiming of space by cliques.

Then there is maintenance. Run your hand under the booth table at your local greasy spoon. Well, don't actually do that—it's disgusting. Your hand is likely to catch on gum, wads of paper, and generally inexplicable gunk. Not to mention the carving of names on booth tables. A booth invites this much in the same way that bean bags call out for the Evil Kenevil in all of us.

As I said at the start, there are many adherents to the booth concept, and there are solid, good reasons to be loyal to the booth concept, but for the money, both up front and over time, there are some better ways to go.

PRESERVING THE DÉCOR

Library designers and architects are meticulous. They strive to create a living space that can adapt to fit the growing needs of communities while delivering a product that meets all the current desires of the library's patrons. Chairs are chosen for comfort and to meet Americans with Disabilities Act (ADA) standards. Aisles need to be wide enough to accommodate patrons in wheelchairs and those pushing strollers. Time is spent considering how best to lay out a department to maximize reference responses and minimize waste.

So why is it that spaces for teens so often clash or stick out?

Ostensibly, the logic is that by making the young adult area unique, you give teens ownership over the space, a place of their own in the library that is set off from the rest of the space, a room of one's own, if you will.

But is this really a good thing?

WELCOME TO ADULTHOOD

Trying to convey this idea without sounding like an angry and bitter old man is a challenge, but I'm going to try. Young adults are not being taught to be better young adults; they are being raised to eventually join the adult world. The progression from infant to child to older child to young adult is a process of refinement, development, and growth into the "final form," if you'll pardon the slightly sci-fi wording, of adulthood.

So why then should young adult spaces be sectioned off entirely, a wholly separate world from both the children's section and the adult's?

As a young college student I had a professor who was in love with the word "liminal," or the state of being "in-between." It was a class in African women's literature, and my professor loved explaining how the authors we were reading spoke from a "liminal" space and how their narratives were "liminal," and even how the landscape of Africa was "liminal" during this "liminal" time and "liminal" place in the "liminal" world. A fellow student and I came to the conclusion that if she you replaced "liminal" with one of George Carlin's "seven words you can't say on television," she'd have been dragged away by campus police.

That said, all young adults are in a liminal state. They are not adults and not children; they are between both of those, often rigidly thought of, concepts. So in creating a space, it would be ideal to embrace both the best of past (childhood) and the future (adulthood), rather than emphasizing their between-ness or liminality, if you will. (I'll only use the word just once more, I promise.)

THE "LITTLE KIDS' ROOM" HORROR

Want to start a fight with a young adult? I don't know why you would, but let's say you're ornery and looking for a fight. Call them a "kid." Go on, give it a go. Actually don't, I really can't afford the lawsuit.

Nothing makes a young person recoil more than reminding them of their youth, just as nothing makes adults more uncomfortable than realizing the maturity inherent in teens. Sending a young adult to a "little kids' room" is like handing a linebacker the keys to a Big Wheel—it's an awkward fit.

A firsthand account I can convey, with grim humor now that the years have piled up between the event and today, was my high school book club being crowded into a room covered in "Rainbow Brite" wall graphics and coloring sheets done by a class of pre-kindergarteners. I was 14 at the time and a large 14. Sitting on a chair that would be generously described as "twee" while talking about Hunter Thompson's *Fear and Loathing in Las Vegas* ranks as one of the more surreal events of my adolescence.

Avoiding such clashes and welcoming young adults into the space fully is a challenge. How do we communicate what is, and is not, for a given group of patrons?

1,001 COLLECTIONS

What's cooler than stickers? They're an instant message from a time before instant messaging. A scrap of paper and glue that conveys a plethora of information about your musical tastes, your crushes, your favorite activities, political opinions, and even your sense of humor. I cover my computers in stickers even as a sour old grown-up. I think of it as "mining" the box, claiming it away from tacky logos. Why should the first thing someone sees when they look over at me typing away be "TOSHIBA" or the ubiquitous Apple logo with a bite missing?

Labeling books with stickers is handy and seems, on the surface, cool. After all, you're creating a unique young adult collection; you're allowing teens to claim these works and authors as their own. Slapping a "YA" sticker on the spine helps the shelvers too, keeps the collection overlap to a minimum, all sound-as-a-pound thinking. That's the epitome of good practice right? Not always.

I'm not simply arguing against the notion of labeling books with categories, after all that is, in some respects, what librarianship stands for—the orderly organization of knowledge. Making books easier to find and easier to organize is a core mission for any kind of librarian. What does rattle the cage a bit is the excessive subdivision of young adult literature and nonfiction.

For example, there is a library in Illinois that has "Young Adult" stickers. They also have stickers for "Sci-Fi" and "Romance" and "New Fiction" and "High Interest" and "Action" and "Mystery." Some books even have multiple stickers, such as the sci-fi, action, young adult novel *Be More Chill*, by Ned Vizzini. Arguably the book, which chronicles the life of a young man with a computer chip in his brain that makes him cooler and more attractive to girls, also has a subtext of romance, but to label it as romance would mean having four stickers on one book. Thankfully, common sense prevailed, and it was only labeled with three: sci-fi, new fiction, and young adult.

At its core, the idea of stickering books is very sound. By drawing in young adult readers and focusing their attention on genres they are familiar with, you increase readership overall. Extra stickers in special sections, displays, and spinner rack segregation—it gets to be too much very quickly.

So what is the best course of action? Keep it simple. Nothing is cooler than simplicity. Marking young adult books as YA is fine, but then leave it be. Getting too involved in what a book is about, or who the book will appeal to or whether it fits into a genre (is *Harry Potter* fantasy or romance or mystery or all three?) creates boundaries. Teen and young adults seek to define themselves in their own terms; trying to do it for them will only backfire.

BIBLIOGRAPHIC INSTRUCTION: THE EASY WAY

Sadly, that sub-heading is a bit of a lie. There is no easy bibliographic instruction. Even the most committed and ardent librarian will confess that sitting down to read a hot pile of notes on shelving and proper library use was not the highlight, whiz-band thrill of library school. I remember an instructor confessing that he loved the Dewey decimal system but that his love was "unrequited, at best."

I've made games of bibliographic instruction, and I've tried to sneak it into tours and talks about library use without talking about library use, all to some success, but it's never easy.

Why? Simply put, getting young people to think about the Dewey decimal system require them to think in a completely new way. Having spilled a great deal of ink on the subject of the elasticity of the young mind prior to this, you may be wondering why making young people think in a new way is a problem? But you're not just asking them to think in a new way, you're asking them to stop thinking in the old way, to abandon their own methods and trust in yours. Of course the truth will win out, and they eventually see how much easier it is to use the catalog than wander the stacks for hours on end searching, in vain, for the one true book that will guide them home again.

But let's not look on that bleak mental image; let's talk about the easy way. It's a system I like to call *passive bibliographic instruction.*

1. Model Building

In your young adult space, you can create a microcosm of the entire library. By avoiding stickers and stickies and gimmicky furniture, you offer an adult experience of the library on a young adult scale. Look at the teen space as a sort of model library, a bit smaller in scale and focused on one group, but comprised of the same materials and resources.

2. Encouraging Independence

The liminal state between childhood and adulthood is frightening, but it's less so when the encouragement is not to dwell in teendom well into your thirties, but rather to grow up and out and engage the wider world. Displays and racking are great on a small scale, but don't let your shelving talk down to teens. Encourage them to work with librarians, but build in easy "instructables" to each interaction. Give a kid a fish, and they'll ask "why did you give me this fish?" Teach a teen to fish, and they'll respect you for a lifetime.

3. Intuitive Feeling

The first night in a new apartment is hell on your toes. That 2 A.M. trip to the bathroom usually means more than a few coins are going in the swear jar. That bewilderment and angry confusion is how many teens feel when wandering the stacks. They know the books are there, they just don't know where this "there" place is and how to get to it. Designing spaces with this in mind is a challenge but it's not impossible. Think about necessity. Dictionaries, encyclopedias, and other ready reference should be grouped together, easy to access, and always in the same place. Making the basic books easy to find goes a long way in helping teens feel comfortable in the space.

THE LITTLE KIDS' ROOM

There's a moment when a parent realizes that their son or daughter is changing faster than their expectations. Perhaps it's when Dad reaches for a picture book only to get the death stare from his little girl. Or when Mom grabs a pile of *Goosebumps* only to be sniffed at and told "those are for babies." Some parents take this in stride, accept it as part of the process, but some try to hold on to the past for nostalgia's sake and go into denial. The latter group can make the horrible mistake of trying to pigeonhole their tween or teen, but to do so is comforting for the parents, while it can make the young adult feel trapped in a cage.

The children's department or Little Kids' Room is the library equivalent of this cage.

A LUCKY PROBLEM

Many reading this might roll their eyes. "I wish we had that problem, we don't even have an activity room!" they say, cursing and tossing the book aside. But wait, even if you don't have a dedicated activity space in mind, there's still the dread possibility of creating a Little Kids' Room in even the most open and unforgiving of floor plans.

I put the term in caps because like a disease or disaster it's a term worthy of respecting, even fearing. The Little Kids' Room is a space in the library that might as well have "Forbidden Zone" painted on wooden slats across the door. Charlton Heston could be wandering, shirtless, on horseback, in a loincloth in this room. Mr. Heston could discover that "They blew it up, you maniacs, you blew it up" and pound the sand before a ruined Statue of Liberty. Yes, it could be as off-putting as ham-handed *Planet of the Apes* references.

THE PAINTED CASTLE

The Little Kids' Room is easy to spot, but hard to define. So, let's look to the librarian's bane, television. A show of some renown in recent years is ABC's *Extreme Home Makeover*. Unlike most reality television, which specializes in destroying people's lives, *Extreme Home Makeover* is generous, to a fault.

The premise is dirt simple. The plucky builders and designers select a telegenic and needy family from obscurity and rebuild their home to fantastic proportions. Great rooms, enormous entertainment centers, kitchens that would shame Julia Child are par for the course. But the children receive the most "special" attention.

Does little Christopher like racecars? Good, because now he sleeps in one. A real F1 racer kitted out with a bedroll. Is Melissa a fan of dinosaurs? Well then, she's going to love being rocked to sleep in the arms of T-Rex animatronic creature now isn't she? Entire rooms built to a theme, filled with an idea of what childhood was or what it is for the particular young person on the show. It's wistful and delightful, but in three years when Melissa is deeply politically active, she's going to be galled by the state of her room. Or in six months when Christopher is wild about horses, he'll roll his eyes every time he curls up in his finely tuned European sports . . . er . . . bed.

The problem with these, very well-meaning to be sure, designs is they lock children into a specific set of parameters. They define childhood by an immediate interest as opposed to a progression, ever upwards and onwards, toward adulthood.

By defining a space for a single age bracket, say kids from 1 to 5 years old or middle schoolers, you do a disservice to those children as they age. The room they once used gladly in third grade now feels awkward and "for little kids." For teenagers this reaction is even more intense, bordering on revulsion.

Understanding young adults is all right there in the label. They are viewed as more mature ("adults") but also reminded of their youth and inexperience ("young") on a regular basis. It's the struggle of their age, to be more adult or more childlike. The powerful attraction of both these positions makes for a great deal of tension. Tension that can be exacerbated by a space that feels designed for their past, doesn't embrace their present, and seems to indicate that their future is all-too distant.

In making a room for teens being mindful of their ever-shifting interests, their evolving fascinations and their nearly constant state of change can be a daunting. How do you make a singular space that serves the needs of a patron base that is constantly evolving?

The first step is to avoid the tender trap of the Little Kids' Room. Appealing as a mural of Peter Rabbit, rainbows, and frolicking anthropomorphic kittens might be to a seven-year-old, it's like kryptonite to that child just a scant five years later.

We'll talk more later about how to design a transformative space, but understanding that rooms that too closely identify with just one age bracket younger can be counterproductive is a huge first step.

We associate rooms with ages. A nursery, a hospice, and a classroom filled with wee desks all give us a sense of who belongs here by subtle visual clues. Being aware of just those clues is vital.

Without being pedantic, here are some questions to ask when evaluating the age range of a space:

- Are the characters or other decorations appealing to patrons of all ages?
- Are seats and surfaces built to a scale that would be comfortable for a range of patrons?
- Does the space seem dedicated to a single, age-based activity (story time or lap sit)?
- Does the room have a "default state"?

The final question is the most critical. Even if you don't have the time or budget to dedicate to developing a devoted young adult space, you can always creation a default state to a room.

What I mean by default state is a room that is unadorned, basic, and spare. The room can be adapted to host a poetry slam, decorated to celebrate Dia de los Muertos, and serve as a meeting room for the library board. Though, one would hope, not all in the same day. A default state can seem spare, but it's best to look at is as a blank canvas, an opportunity for young adults to self-define the space as the activities with it occur.

THE NAME IS THE GAME

As a child growing up in the 1980s and 1990s, I was robbed of my library. Like faerie folk, the thieves left a changeling child in its place. "The Learning Center" and "The Information Center" replaced the simple, and descriptive, library. Some view the word *library* as old-fashioned, even archaic.

Rather than engaging lengthy diversion as to the importance of the word library, its place in history, its power and prestige as a concept, I'll simply say these people are wrong. A learning center is a vague concept. Can one *not learn* in the learning center? Can you just grab magazine and grab some floor in the learning center? Would you be stopped? Are you being watched? Are there library police? I mean, are there learning center police? Information center is even vaguer. I envision a poorly staffed kiosk made of cheap plastic.

Names matter. They not only give a sense of what a place is to the patron, they can actually define the space. Let's look at three real examples of young adult spaces. Each of these is commonly used and, though this is a critique, were clearly chosen with good intentions.

Teen Zone

Zone, as a word, has a wonderful science fiction feel to it. It harkens back to *The Twilight Zone*. It give sense of oddness, due in no small part to its use of the letter Z. But, with all apologies to the late Rod Serling, zones don't have a very good feel to them in the real world. Korea is divided by the "Demilitarized Zone," and the area surrounding Chernobyl, an irradiated landscape, is called the "Zone of Alienation." Again, the good intentions are quite clear, creating a space that feels "cool" and "hip" by giving it a name that seems to harken to the oblique and strange is understandable, but it's more likely to raise giggles from teens.

Teen Spot

Your average teen might not think of Samuel Pepys, famed diarist of 17th-century London upon seeing this name, but it definitely puts me in mind of the man who witnessed the Great Fire of London firsthand and lived to write about it. *Spots* were, for centuries, a gentile way of speaking of "lesions" and "sores." A spot feels fixed ("Stay in this spot!") and less than inclusive.

Teen Area

Imagine, if you will, a droning voice informing you that "this, this is our teen area. It has many pleasant activities for the young adult. The area features materials. It also features lighting and assorted furniture. Please follow me to the next area." Calling a space an "area" seems more like a shrug than a carefully chosen title. It also feels defined by the negative, as in, "Why aren't you in the teen area? It's the designated area for your age bracket!"

A GOOD NAME IS A GOOD START

So what should we call the space for young adults? One route is to go corporate. Rather than incorporate "teen" into the name, create a unique brand for your community. Say that your town or neighborhood is famed for its Bur Oak trees. The Bur Oak's Latin name is *Quercus macrocarpa*, and they have some of the largest acorns of any oak. So what if you called your teen area "Macros" or "The Acorn" or even "The Bur"? It's not completely obvious, it encourages people to ask about the name, and it gives you an in to sell the space to the curious.

Another route is to allow teens to name the space themselves, through a contest or teen advisory committee. The library can hold open nominations, have teens put any suggestion in a drop box, and then do some round robin voting to narrow it down. Outside of pruning out some of the more, shall we say, evocative, suggestions keeping adult involvement to a minimum helps young adults feel that the space is their own.

Perhaps a more radical suggestion is not to have a name at all. Simply by grouping materials into an area, placing comfortable furniture and letting it be, the space creates its own identity.

Returning again to the notion of not dividing the collection up too much, is naming a particular space just a more physical form of collection division? The crux of the argument for creating a young adult space at all, let alone defining it by name, lies in the admission that teens make use of both adult and children's materials and that their own materials would not find purchase in either entirely. Defining the young adult space as a wholly distinct one, a named and definite territory, can go a long way in bolstering teen library use.

Territory is another word that is not used lightly. Think of the library as the world entire, a global community. Each area, children's, adult, reference, and young adult, is a nation unto itself, a singular land defined as much by the people who use it as the topography. In this, rapidly belabored metaphor, the ideal world contains nations who are at peace with one another, trade with one another, and allow citizens free passage between all countries. But nations are tricky things. The people of a nation can become swollen with pride, even hubris, which can lead to self-definition at the expense of others. Here it is that the librarian plays the role of the United Nations. By helping each community, each nation within the library, to have a strongly defined sense of space, collection, and purpose, why, you could have peace on earth. Well, library earth anyway.

3

◇ ◇ ◇

MORE THAN MEETS THE EYE

In the 1980s there was one television show that, above all others, combined children's interests in technology, large objects, and colorful characters. The show was *The Transformers*, and its premise (that giant robots hide amongst humanity in the form of vehicles and mechanical devices of all shapes and sizes) made it an enormous hit. The tag line for the Transformers brand was "More than meets the eye." A child could imagine riding in a car one moment and atop an enormous metal robot the next. This basic idea connected with the primal urge to create something new out of the ordinary.

While young adults may have grown beyond the target demographic for the Transformers, they are still captivated by the idea of transformation and change in their daily lives. Take as an example a classroom assignment wherein students are allowed to reposition their desks and chairs to work in groups. No two groupings will be completely alike even if the number of students is constant. Groups will form based on social hierarchy, personal interactions, and preferences in terms of space within the room; the prize space is the one with the most autonomy from the teacher or other groups. Allowing students to reorganize their daily environment allows them a whole new outlet for creativity and social networking.

Within the typical library setting, a sense of uniformity is often given priority over creative expression. Tables and chairs are ordered based on their comfort, durability, and affordability not for their "curb appeal," as it were. In using the library furniture, patrons of all ages are often discouraged from moving things around, usually due to safety and access concerns.

With young children, a sense of transformative space is easy to accomplish: simply shove aside any furniture and hunker down on the floor. This can still work with teens of course, but designing a space with the transformational element already in place can yield even better results.

WHAT FURNITURE SAYS

If you dropped someone off in a random apartment, assuming you do such strange things as kidnap strangers and dump them in other strangers homes, and asked them to discern the age of the inhabitants, one of the first clues would be the furniture.

A college student's furniture often embraces two qualities—cheap and "eclectic." I place the word *eclectic* in quotes because it is simply a euphemism for weird. The large purple velvet chaise next to the leopard print couch set off by the antique apothecary chest are all brought together by the large poster of a marijuana leaf. A cobbling of cheap and free items in pursuit of an identity is the sum of a college student's home. I write this as a recovering grad student who may or may not have had an orange felt lounger held together with bailing wire and prayer in my room.

As one acquires money and, perhaps, taste, the furniture develops an aesthetic. Some might adopt trends or hew close to certain brands. How often have you seen the apartment of a twentysomething that appears to be the exploded remnants of an IKEA? As we age, our furnishings speak to our own history, an accumulation of personal artifacts that might range from banal materials to cherished objects.

The common wisdom would seem to indicate that a common, public space would lack personal connection, that a space developed to be used by all can be, ultimately, claimed by none. How personal a space is is often used to measure the suitability of a space for public use. Is this space non-specific enough? Does it appeal to everyone, or better stated, anyone? Does the furniture say anything when it is meant to say nothing at all?

FLIMSY AND MOBILE: A QUESTION OF FURNITURE

I mentioned IKEA previously, and it's for good reason: the Swedish furniture retailer, founded in 1943, is the world's largest furniture manufacturer. Their so-called flat-pack method of shipping furniture has won them design acclaim and innumerable fans among those who want to save some money on delivery but don't mind assembling their furniture on their own.

But just as not every person who cracks a copy of the *Dewey Decimal Classification* (DDC) is not a librarian, not everyone who wields the ubiquitous multi-tool of IKEA is a carpenter. While the Swedish designs might be ideal if assembled with care and patience, college students with short attention spans tend to devote less than the necessary amount of love and concern to the building process. The end result is all too often shelves with a more than is healthy amount of sway and "extra pieces."

Libraries are not dorm rooms to twentysomething flop pads. They are institutions that have to adhere not only to local health and safety laws but the ADA (Americans with Disabilities Act) and OSHA (Occupational Health and Safety Administration) laws, neither of which, one might imagine, have much tolerance for "extra pieces."

Creating light and mobile furniture for a teen space is essential. The ability to rearrange a space, to customize it to suit specific programming needs as well as the ever-evolving temperament of young adults is huge challenge. Asking even the most hale and hearty staff to heft around booth seating and heavy tables is just asking for a revolt, or worse yet, an injury. So the balance must be struck between flimsiness and mobility.

One way to solve this problem is sticking to simplicity. It may sound pedantic, but what's wrong with a solid table and a few chairs? Creating a unique space for teenage patrons doesn't mean you have to sacrifice the aesthetic of the library as a whole. In fact, by incorporating the space into the library plan while at the same time setting it off with touches of individual style, teenagers feel both welcomed and addressed as patrons.

DECORATION: CLAIMING A SPACE

I will confess that as a young adult I tormented my sainted Irish mother with a design sense that would have made the Sex Pistols turn up their noses. There was a duct tape anarchy symbol in which the cross of the *A* was formed with a black armband from the comic book issue memorializing the death of Superman. There was the glow-in-the-dark skull and ghoul poster phase. There were several years when various quotes from sources including Ayn Rand, G. K. Chesterton, and Hawkeye from *M*A*S*H* could be found on my walls scrawled in white-out. I treated my 1990s teenage domain as a cross between an art studio and a hobo flop. And it all started with the bicycle wallpaper.

I'd been stuck with this horrid patter of old time bicycle wallpaper (the kind with the huge wheel in front and tiny wheel behind) for years. I viewed it as nothing less than an affront to my artistic integrity. I believe at some point I may have actually uttered the words "this is an affront to my artistic integrity" to adults who were kind enough not to laugh at me. I hated that wallpaper. It was "kiddie" wallpaper. I was not longer a kid. I was 12 years old. Pardon. I was "12 years old dammit!" was how I would have put it at the time.

This precocious trot down embarrassing memory lane serves to open a discussion of decoration of a teen library space, and just how long and strange a trip that might be for a library.

Let's first discuss materials. When we talk about decoration, we're generally talking about paint, paper, art supplies. More exotic materials can include canvas, glass, wire, metal, the stuff of creation, and the matter of art. Allowing teenagers to self-define in a space is a wonderful opportunity to let art happen. If that has the patina of the "hippie" on it, don't be too alarmed. There is value in letting kids' freak flags fly and simply handing them the tools of creation.

Create a paper dragon that hangs from a drop ceiling and bears the name of every youth volunteer. Set up a constantly evolving mural of graffiti art or a message board, a sort of lo-fi Twitter™ that can only be written on in the form of a rebus. These are just a few of possibilities for ongoing decorative pieces to add to any teen library space.

Decoration should be collaborative, about building community, sharing ideas, and showcasing talent. Invite the teen who says they "can't draw" to help the artist with ideas. Giving direction on the form and shape of the project is good, but let the young adults complete the project on their own steam. Nothing stings worse for a young adult than having an idea rejected, especially by an adult, when it applies to their peer group.

CLASSIC, NOT MOMENTARY

The grips of teenage fads are something we will touch on time and time again but it goes without saying that even the savviest librarian can be left gobsmacked, as the British would say, in the face of the tides and trends of teenage fashion. Trying to keep up with the fickle natures of teenagers has even spawned an entire profession: cool hunting, the hunt to keep up with the slightest tremor of trend among teenagers.

Cool hunters are trendspotters. William Gibson immortalized the profession in his book *Pattern Recognition*. The cool hunter Cayce Pollard's unique talent was to be able sense the inherent "coolness" of brands. In real life, cool hunters look at street art, garage rock, indy publishing, and daring fashion to find out what is going to be the next big thing. Any cool hunter worth their salt looks to teenagers and young adults as a veritable cornucopia of coolness. Teenagers define the hippest fashions before, as, and even after they have happened in everything form from music to clothing to language itself.

In college and grad school I made extra money working for a consumer survey organization that showcased new products, television shows, and even food items to young adults. In one instance a candy company had paid an enormous amount of money to showcase a new kind of Halloween gross-out candy. Eyeballs filled with raspberry jam and fingers that seemed to gush a lemon-flavored pus were just a couple of examples. In 15 separate seminars I watched kids from ages 12 to 17 pick up these gross candies, handle them for a few moments, throw them at each other, smash them into the table, and put back the ruined remnants in the bowl.

It was only when we pointed out that they were candy that they actually tasted them.

Without a signifier, a guidepost, a clear idea of what a thing is and how it works, only the most intuitive space is going to be accessible to a teen audience. Creating a teen space that is, for instance, devoid of books with an emphasis on computer stations and study carrels begs the question from the teens: "Isn't this the library?"

The danger is in playing with form so much, and so wildly, that the basic function behind the form is lost. There is no shame in emphasizing literature, reading for pleasure and plain old, good old, old-old fashioned books.

Take a moment to consider the much-maligned book as a form. Technology seems to scoff at the capacity of a book, which might come in at the same mass and weight as a laptop but contain considerably less information. How many times have you see the image of some huge tome, or stack of tomes next to a single disc or thumb drive? It's the stuff of advertising clichés (to paraphrase the Genie from Disney's *Aladdin* describing his life in the lamp): "Unbelievable cosmic power! Itty-bitty living space."

Emphasizing the wonder that can be found in books, the classic format of words on the printed page, is something that libraries looking to capture a teen audience should never lose sight off. Chasing the ephemeral technologically minded young adult with no use for books is a game of shadow tag.

THE CLUTCH OBJECT

If the Harry Potter and Twilight series have taught libraries anything, it is the power of the clutch object. Observe the fan of any of these generation-defining books, and you will see them holding on to the latest tome or tomes in these series for dear life. Whether on the first read through, or the nostalgic 50th visitation to the hallways of Hogwarts, there is way that the teen reader holds their book near and dear that is wholly a young adult phenomenon.

As is often the case, this is a matter of personal definition. Like clothing, hairstyle, or slang, the items one surrounds oneself with define one's character, radiating a sense of personal identity as clearly as any slogan or pop song. The film *High Fidelity*, based on the Nick Hornsby book of the same name, tackled this idea. In the modern era, what you like (be it music, books, movies) defines you as much as anything. Someone who says they like "music" and reads "books" almost certainly sets off alarm bells for even the most casual questioner. We want to know what you like, because it helps us understand you better, and perhaps even get a sense of whether we are compatible with you.

The physical book is a powerful talisman of personality. A *Buffy the Vampire Slayer* graphic novel conveys not just a fascination with the humorously occult, but quite possibly a love for all things created by writer/director Joss Whedon. A man who created television shows about empowered demon slayers (*Buffy*), ensouled vampires (*Angel*), rebel space cowboys (*Firefly*), and mind-hacked human "dolls" (*Dollhouse*) has created something of a cargo cult, to the point where T-shirts reading "Joss Whedon Is My Master" can be spotted on fans worldwide. That Buffy graphic novel might tell you a great deal indeed.

In many respects, tapping into the clutch impulse is a key way librarians can define a space for teens. How does one translate the personal totem to the defined space as a whole? How can we take that simple impulse and expand it to help create attractive and evolving spaces for teens? One simple way is to create spaces that feel malleable and, in some fashion, portable. This begins with a collection that is in constant evolution, yet also stable.

EVOLVING, BUT STABLE

It's a common sight to any young adult librarian, the stack of books piled high in the hands of an eager young patron. Whether it is a selection of graphic novels, every vampire heartthrob book, or a trove of chemistry books, the hoard in the hands is something almost every young adult patron will have sooner or later. Whether these items are collected for a school assignment or just simple curiosity, there's a passion to gathering as much as possible, to diving deep into the collection and "mining" the materials.

The word *mining* here has more than the usual connotation. First, the obvious: those young adult patrons are attempting to gather as much richness as they can from a collection. The pride of any youth services department is their ability to respond to the needs of a patron base with a depth of materials on a range of subjects. Whether this means developing a biography section that covers local sports heroes and topical musicians and performers or developing the comics and graphic novel section to lead from the most popular of superhero books into the deeper and more nuanced works in the medium, developing a rich "vein" of library material is the good and heeded work of any library staff.

Mining goes beyond that simple metaphor when it comes to developing a space for young adults. To better understand what I mean it would behoove me to talk about Fred Wilson.

Mr. Wilson is a conceptual artist whose work has been lauded as revolutionary both in it's concept and context. He is a recipient of prestigious Macarthur Foundation Genius Grant. For you see, while you might very well find Mr. Wilson's work in a museum, you're not going to find it hanging limply on a wall or roped off by careful docents. No, Mr. Wilson's work is in fact the museum exhibition itself.

In one of his seminal works, titled "Mining the Museum," Wilson worked with Maryland Historical Society's collection. Wilson's work often tackles the difficult subject of race and racial injustice. In this exhibition, Wilson used objects from the collection in juxtaposition to show the parallel narratives of life in Baltimore over the centuries, in white and black communities. A photograph of slaves was placed next to 20th-century ceramic toy charactitures of African Americans. A baby's carriage from the 1920s with a Klansman's hood placed inside was a harrowing reminder of the prominence of that organization during that era. Wooden Cigar Store "Indians" were turned to face away from the patron, as if ashamed. All of these materials were from the collection, all of them represented the history, culture, and people's of the area to some extent or another, and yet when placed in these new, often jarring contexts, they opened up whole new avenues of discussion.

Wilson's work might be a bit more provocative than the average teen space in a library would be looking for, of course, but the core ideas of creating a collection in the space that provokes discussion and evolves with the young adult audience is a sound one.

Let's start with a current, and perennial, favorite of young adult collections—graphic novels. Many libraries already pull graphic novels and place them in their own stand-alone section. This is done for a variety of reasons. First and foremost, the popularity of graphic novels makes them a great draw in for young adult audiences. Seeing a large display of the graphic novel selection is an excellent way to increase foot traffic. Second, graphic novels' size and shape can vary quite a bit from traditional novels and nonfiction. Western (American) graphic novels are often larger, thinner and "floppier." Manga, or Amerimanga, are fatter and resemble a tradition massmarket paperback. Graphic novels, especially manga and American superhero books, often run in series. Having the collections all together is good shelving practice in that respect.

But how can a graphic novel collection be organized such that it evolves with and provokes the audience? Many libraries group manga with books about Japanese culture and design. Technological superhero books like *Iron Man* might be grouped with nonfiction on current generation robotics, artificial intelligence, and movie making. As cliché as it might sound, some librarians could group *Spider-Man* alongside books about arachnids.

As discussed previously, the notion of creating an endless series of sticker subsets is not appealing. It's messy and disorderly, and it ultimately divides up a solid collection into nigh disorder. So how can we create a collection space that can responds rapidly to young adult patron's constantly shifting interests but that doesn't cause a shelving nightmare or simply a big mess? The answer may lie in a drop zone.

DROP ZONES

The best piece of advice I received as a nascent librarian was how to work a book truck. One of my first library positions was as an assistant. I held no degree, had no "authority," and was often the catch-as-catch-can for any and all drudgework. Need a thousand tiny paper fish cut? I was your man. Need M&M'S® sorted by color for a mathematics program? I got down to sorting. While the work was not quite fighting for the great glory of Sparta at Thermopylae, it taught me the value of learning every nuance of a library. Book trucks were a part of my education.

At this library, unsorted books were collected on book trucks and tucked away until sorted for reshelving. The shelvers were often overwhelmed by the sheer volume of children's and young adult books that drifted from shelves to tables, so there was often a backlog of books that needed to be shelved. Sorting a book truck is not a work of joy, even for the most committed librarian, or a librarian in most dire need of commitment. You begin by trying to parse out some manner of order, perhaps all the *A* authors here, or the *G* authors there. Then suddenly, a rich and deep vein of nonfiction titles or cheap and authorless 1970s *Doctor Who* paperbacks, all listed with some arcane code number for the spinner racks, appears. And let us not even speak of the board books, their edges chewed raw. Oh, the humanity.

The finest librarian I knew, a gentleman named Ron, would urge me to look at this soul-sucking work as a learning experience. "You're handling the collection. It's all passing through your fingers. Tactile knowledge." He was spot-on. By the time I'd been in the job six months, I had a sense of the collection bordering on the eerie. Someone could describe a book and I started to just "know." It's a truism in many libraries, but the shelvers, especially those vested souls who have been at it for decades, have a knowledge of the collection that far surpasses we know-it-all librarians. In the military, this position is called "the ground situation."

I mention all this as preface to any radical suggestion I make in regards to shelving practices because I know the horror. I've seen seven book trucks filled up after a sustained three-day weekend before science fair. They may not sing sagas or hold a place in Valhalla for those brave souls who charge into that work, but they should.

Put simply, a drop zone is a deliberate attempt to maintain disorder within the collection. A vague and wild space intentionally held in the midst of orderly LOC (Library of Congress) and Dewey. Creating one or several drop zones in a teen library space could, if done well, provide a contextual platform for not only the most current materials but also connect young adult patrons to materials deeper in the collection than they might normally be tempted to go.

HOW TO DO THIS AND NOT GO MAD

Librarians by nature are orderly. From the clean straight lines of books on the shelves to rows of shelves themselves, there is a sweet poetry in well-organized information. Creating a space where materials have some wiggle room has always been a part of library best practices. It's nothing new to create a display of materials themed around a current event or topic. When a hugely popular book flies in and on then off the shelves, it's only good form to move books in the same vein (perhaps all too literal vein if we speak of the glittering vampires of the Twilight series) and highlight those materials. But these are temporary movements, often lasting only so long as the passing reader's interest.

The concept behind a drop zone is to create a stable medium between more traditional shelving practices and more open and evolving space plan. The key word here is *evolving*. I've used it a number of times very specifically. Evolution is an immutable process here, deeply at work in the library.

A quick Darwinian side step. Evolution is not a linear process. For every successful species, every successful organism, history is littered with a billion failures. Darwin's *Origin of the Species* most offended Victorians not because of it's possibly irreligious content, but because it portrayed nature as ambivalent. The survival of the fittest, the struggle of all species in a great game of life, was bestial and even barbaric to the genteel Victorian mind. Put a bit less dramatically, evolution is kind of messy.

Drop zones are meant to be messy areas. High-interest, high-impact fiction and nonfiction placed in areas at the heart of a teen section. Many of the books might be new releases, current "hot" books, books being adapted to films. Music or films that are new or enjoying a revival, the usual stuff of a New Releases shelf. The drop zone concept goes beyond this, cutting deeper into the collection, mining it.

As an example, the Ember series by Jeanne DuPrau features a postapocalyptic world in which the last human city is winding down. The first book in the series was adapted into a film. Placing the books in the series with the film is a first step. Add postapocalyptic books like *A Canticle for Leibowitz* or *The Stand* or video games such as the Fallout series or Bioshock even tabletop games like Rifts or Dead Reign. Now build out on that theme with books on survivalist, urban gardening, and futurist thinking. Add relevant printed articles, magazines from the serials collection, even list of Web sites and online materials.

All those materials were built off one "clutch" book.

The key to a drop zone is a temporary tag, whether electronic or physical that puts the materials in the area for a given time. It can be as simple as a notation in the catalog. The idea is to keep the material in the drop zone and circulating back as long as the mini-collection lasts.

Again, how does this differ from a display? Displays, while attractive and good for highlighting material, are often pulled apart by passing readers too quickly to reach maximum impact. The casual and clutch nature of the young adult reader requires something meatier than a simple stand-up book display. Displays are also just that, for display.

They lack often lack the power to connect with the audience and are bypassed.

Developing a micro-collection that connects and responds to current reading trends is one way to show a rapid and evolving understanding of young adults interests. Ideally, a drop zone might be revised every 2–3 weeks, perhaps even more often, if demand is high enough. Developing a simple and straightforward means of tracking materials and keeping them in the designated area (without driving shelving librarians to distraction) means that the speed of response can be as quick as the interest. A sudden interest in a new location featured on a reality show or a resurgence of interest in punk music thanks to the soundtrack of a given film— even the most passing of fancies can be tapped and mined to highlight the collection.

One additional benefit is the creation of a "hook" for frequent patrons. If drop zones are done well, they can create a constantly churning new idea space. A teen coming in one week might find a wealth of information about a current election or national debate. The next week, a look a current styles and their roots in history and fashion.

Perhaps the most exciting aspect of drop zones is the notion of letting teens design and create the packages themselves. It could be an activity that your Teen Advisory Council takes up, or it could be a means by which you start a Teen Advisory Council. Ask for input from frequent patrons, or hold a contest to design the drop zone space and pick the first topics. The possibilities for opening up the process, and thus completing a circuit of interactivity and interconnectedness with teens and young adults, are endless.

THEY'RE ONLY GOING TO CHEAT

Sooner or later, every librarian runs into a crab. No, I don't mean the crustacean or any cartoon variation of the same. I refer instead to someone who, either as a patron or co-worker, has a sour and dour take on teens and young adults. Often this is someone who will regale you with tales of terror about how "disrespectful" teenagers can be. They bemoan the great lost time when young adults were quiet and showed deference. Most wise librarians give these Debbie Downers about as much mental headspace as tales about walking uphill to school, both ways, in the snow with no shoes . . . and liking it.

These grouses will no doubt look at any effort to evolve the collection or disrupt the sainted order of the shelves as everything from "catering to the lowest common denominator" to "failing to teach good bibliographic skills" to out-and-out blasphemy. Shaking their copies of the DDC they will bemoan the lack of standards. And how did skirts get so short, and why are the hippies and their music ever so loud?

The purpose of the collection is to serve the patron. The ordering and classification of knowledge makes that job easier, both for patrons and for library staff. Librarians have been pulling books off the shelves and out of place to excite young readers for ages. Creating spaces of fun within the library itself can provide a sense of possibility in the random. In a sense, a drop zone allows a library to brand their collection and to use current trends, topics, passions, and fashions to plumb the shelves for material that might otherwise get over looked or passed over.

The library as monolith is appealing on some level. The great mahogany shelves, the hushed chilling calm of the stacks, a sense of ageless quiet, and almost grim rectitude is one that almost seems to linger in the great subconscious of librarianship. Even the most tech-savvy, over-caffeinated, newly degreed, and Linux-powered librarian savant pines for the great unchanging halls of old. It's a sort of perfection that appeals largely because it never existed, and where it did, good riddance to all that.

A library is a living organism, or perhaps, better stated, a species. With each succeeded generation the struggle is to adapt, evolve, and ultimately survive through the next generation. The old line about hoe "children are our future" sounds like a bit of politician blather, but in terms of an evolving and living institution like a library, it's very true. As our institution evolves, it is in our children, our youngest patrons, that we see new ideas form, reform, take shape, and, in the end, survive or fail.

We are then challenged, like a wild animal in the Darwinian struggle, to be more than meets the eye, to add value while preserving integrity, to create substantive and personal spaces that are accessible to all, and to honor our history while reaching towards the future—to evolve.

4

◇ ◇ ◇

HIGH TEA ON THE
TENNIS COURTS

THE SMUGGLERS

When I was in college, a professor of mine would refer to an incident in
the novel *England, England* by Julian Barnes. In the book, a mad scheme
has been hatched to recreate the entirety of Great Britain in miniature as
an amusement park on the Isle of Wight. The idea of the planners was
that visitors could soak up the whole of British history (castles, cathedrals,
and even great fiction like Robin Hood) in a single visit. My professor was
fond of citing a point in the novel when the fortunes of the theme park
take a dire turn. It is reported that there is a problem with the men hired to
portray smugglers from the imperial past. The problem with the smugglers? It seems they are actually smuggling.

That's as fine a place as any to begin considering the creation of vital
activity and programming spaces for teens and young adults.

It's not an unfair generalization to say that most young adult librarians
view teens through rose-colored glasses. There is something innate in
those who would choose, or sidle into, this corner of the bibliographic
arts that gives them an open mind when it comes to teenagers, a patience
of almost Job-like proportions. Where others might see a motley crew, a

rabble, a mob with mischief in their eyes and terror in their hears, young adult librarians see an opportunity. Get books in their hands; screen movies to get them thinking; organize programming, games, tournaments, events, speakers, book clubs, cooking demonstrations, science demonstrations, anything and everything to channel that youthful energy. The wild and irascible nature of teens is, in truth, the joyous challenge of working with them.

Or perhaps we're all simply a little mad. But in a very good way.

Teenagers are keenly aware of their strength in numbers. Cast your mind back to the poor soul who stepped in to substitute teach in your high school. All manner of deviltry could befall just such an unfortunate. In one of my first positions as a school librarian, I would fill in for exam days or homerooms for absent teachers. I was told that it was common practice for the students to loudly discuss their bodily functions or that Mr. Smith regularly allowed students to watch HBO on the classroom television. While it was generally one clever boy or girl who took the lead in trying to pull a fast one, the whole class would happily fall in. There were moments I imagined that I was experiencing the animal panic of a gazelle on the open plain, spotted by one lion, then two, then the whole pride.

Teenagers will be teenagers, and while that is not as irksome as smugglers, it can prove to be a unique challenge for young adult librarians. This chapter will cover the creation of programming and activity spaces within the library and how those spaces can meet the distinct challenges of serving young adult patrons, challenges that include the self-identification of a space, the ownership of space, the physical requirements of a space, and the possibility of having high tea on a tennis court or serving a buffet to barbarians in a broom closet.

NO ONE LIKES THEIR LITTLE BROTHER

Is that a provocative statement? Perhaps, but I've found it to be true at least part of the time. I won't be so bold as to postulate a percentage of time, but the percentage is not slight. I write this as an only child raised in a single-parent household. Or as my friends with younger siblings used to say, "Oh my god, you are SO lucky!"

While I lacked a sibling, I did have a younger cousin who was attached to my hip for much of my childhood. Charlie delighted in nothing more than the complete humiliation and destruction of anything of value in my life. In many respects, he was a Mongol horde in the form of an eight-year-old boy. I mean that with no insult to the Mongols.

The worst part of living with Charlie was not his tantrums, his deceits, his destruction of my personal property, his thefts, his gambits with the local hooligans that often left me running for my life after allegedly insulting someone's mother or sister, or even (god help me) his body odor after a long hard day of rolling in the mud pits near our homes. No, all of that was just part and parcel of being his older cousin.

It was the sharing. How I loathed the sharing.

As a culture, we try to instill in our children a sense of reverence for the concept of sharing. No matter what is being shared (one's toys, one's food, one's compassion in a time of need), the act of sharing transcends religious and philosophical differences. To share with your family, with your siblings, with your irate and felonious cousin, this is human nobility writ large.

I would have rather tap danced in a minefield.

The worst was sharing activities. If I wanted to go the mall, along came the boy. If I wanted to go to the park, along came the boy. Then one day, everything changed.

I was at my local branch of the Chicago Public Library and saw a notice for a young adult reading group. They were reading George Orwell's classic *1984*. A discussion was planned, two weeks hence. Food and drinks, kids my age and older, teachers, and the greatest words of all "Patrons 12 and older only please." Ha! Freedom!

Finally, there was an event solely for me, shaped for my participation. And no one was going to make me countermand the flyer.

I should say before I move on that Charlie, now Chuck, is a fine young man these days. For all his torments, he was a wonderful little brother substitute. Though to this day, I believe he owes me the chance at least one good sucker punch and at least 40 dollars in arcade tokens.

THE LITTLE KIDS' ROOM

It's nigh an act of alchemy to pinpoint the exact moment when a child becomes a young adult. We can go with the general distinction of having made it to junior high, but there are any number of fifth graders who would beg to differ with that assessment. Nineteen-year-olds are still technically teenagers, but does teen programming aimed at their siblings six years younger (who are also teenagers) cast too wide a net? Regardless of when the strange state of young adulthood begins or ends, one aspect all those within its nebulous confines can agree upon is the discomfort they feel when referred to as "kids"; especially, "little kids."

Unwelcome designations of childhood likely cause more disruptions at family holiday meals than any disagreement over politics or sports combined. Being assigned to the dread "little kids' table" when you are well past the age when devouring paste and not potatoes is a worry. More than anything, young adults wish to be seen as the latter half of that description and not the former. The more rarified the adult air they can breathe in, the better.

So how then do libraries avoid this thorny issue, this taboo trap of patting a burgeoning adult on the head and tut-tutting them back to the cardboard table with sporks and spoons and plastic knives?

The first and easiest way to avoid offending teens is to clearly define, and if possible, separate, young adult and children's spaces within the library. This may sound like a simple notion, but it goes far beyond consulting the layout of the library and finding a corner or two that works best.

Some libraries assign teen services to the adult department, others to the youth services. Some overlap up to a certain age, some just don't assign their staff that specifically. This is a case in which your library or system will be rolling its own. Each of these set-ups presents a unique challenge. In broad terms, let's address each one at a time.

In a system where children's services oversee young adult materials and programming, the goal is create a clear division. Young adults will associate the children's area, whether it's a whole floor, a department, or a wing with the "kids' section" and as they grow older will have difficulty seeing beyond that.

The goal here should be to create as much neutral space as possible. A cleared-out area for teens and young adults that differs both in its design (if possible) as well as its use. Dedicating a room or section solely to young adult activities, even that most basic of young adult activities of "hanging out," is essential to creating a space young adults can feel comfortable in. Even if surrounded by cartoon murals, puzzle kits, and board books, young adults can feel as if a space has been reserved just for them.

Creating a defined programming space could be as simple as clustering furniture from the adult department along with young adult materials. Larger definers, like specialized furniture, games, and electronics, can also wall off the space a bit. There's also a social element to defining areas. Making a conscious effort to hold programming for younger children out of the young adult area, and vice versa of course, is one way to ensure that teens feel at home. Another way is to encourage teens to use the adult and children's areas for socializing or large projects to make use of all the programming space available to them.

When the young adult section falls under adult services, there's often a concern that teen programming and spaces will become unruly or disrupt the often-quiet spaces adults services tend to cultivate.

The advent of big-chain book stores in the 1990s, as well as coffeehouses and cafe culture, has seen a generational shift in how younger generations view public studying. The austere concept of pure and silent contemplation is almost alien to those who grew up studying at Starbucks or meeting friends in the manga aisle at Barnes and Noble.

The cafe approach is one that could work wonders in an adult department playing host to young adult programming. Creating cafe style seating, with a relaxed approach to noise levels, more clustered and communal seating, as well the ability to rework the space as needed for programming events, is ideal. Think of creating a small coffeehouse inside your library dedicated to serving the young adult community.

Finally, there are smaller libraries that perhaps lack the resources or personnel to devote to full-time young adult space. Here, events become all the more important. Make use of any and all available space, even areas of the library not typically used, such as the basement or common areas around the building. These types of spaces could make excellent areas for holding young adult programming on a budget.

When it comes to spending money on a programming space, it's important to note that leafing through library catalogs can often engender quite a bit of "furniture" envy amongst librarians. I can remember my first library supply catalog that was filled with vintage booth seating, great shiftable benches, and track-lit counters for congregating. All of them far in excess of what my department could ever hope to spend. Don't be deterred by a small budget. A great library space for teen programming is not a matter of cash, but of creativity.

Let's talk about big rooms and small rooms and how filling them with exciting programming is less about size than perspective.

THE BIG ROOM

The joke runs thusly: Two dowagers are out on holiday. They stop at a lunch buffet advertising a meal that's far cheaper than anything in town. Rushing in, the two women find that the food is simply dreadful—stale bread, soggy sandwiches, and other dodgy fare. The first woman tries a few dishes before pushing her plate away in disgust. Her companion tucks in with gusto, going back for seconds, and then thirds. The first woman, appalled, asks, "How can you eat this muck? It's dreadful." To which her companion replied "Oh yes, the food is awful, but you can't beat the portions!"

You've been given a big portion, a big room. Perhaps it's the library basement, a Spartan space where you need to bring everything in and out as well as clear clutter. Maybe you've been given access to a large meeting room, complete with chairs and tables, giving you a variety of options. Whatever the taste, you've been given a large portion. Now how to make it work for young adult programming?

The first challenge is maintaining a sense of order and flow. Let's look at that most orderly of spaces that young people spend much of their time in, classrooms.

A classroom has several key features that help define the space without being too overt about it. First, there is the access point. Often there is only one door and if there are two doors, many savvy teachers will block one off. Having one door has two effects: it allows the teacher to monitor who comes and goes at any given time and it gives a sense of clear direction. While most libraries aren't going to chide patrons for having to leave a program early, it's just good form to know who is coming in. This can be very useful for keeping tabs on programming statistics, especially in programs where the attendance can waver.

Then there's the teacher's desk. For every teacher out there, you'll find a different philosophy, but a good solid idea is to make the teacher's desk, or podium, a point of focus for students. It's something in the middle of the room that their desks can be pointed towards. A fixed object in the idea space of the classroom. Find a center for your program, a fixed point to which you can draw attention and shape the furniture and floor plan around that fixed point.

About those desks, they're a challenge in their own right. Being able to slide around, visit friends and boyfriends and girlfriends during class would just be unseemly. Hence, rows. In some programming, neat lines and layouts are a fine thing, but not always. A video game salon or book-binding craft workshop needs to spread out a bit. Again, find a focal point, organize the furniture around that point and realize that clusters of friends, Keep these ideas in mind: a single entrance/exit, possibly with a check-in point; a focal point for the room and furniture that accentuates that focal point without limiting young adults' ability to congregate. So what can you do in a big ol' room?

When programming for young adults, one key aspect is to understand that teenagers are, by nature, enamored of transgressive behavior. The testing of social mores, norms, and boundaries is part and parcel of adolescence. When making use of a large room, the more you can fill it with something unusual, perhaps even daring, the more attention your programming is likely to get. In short, make use of the ceilings; the floors, and everything in between

Let's start up above. At a video game night, setting up cooperative music games like Guitar Hero™, Rock Band™, and Singstar™ on a television can entertain only a set number of participants in one section of the room at a time. Play with the vertical elements in the room is to use creative lighting. Playing around with track lights and lamps can create spotlights. Colored sheets of plastic can mimic gels and create a whole host of concert-like effects. Bathe the room in a rainbow of colors as players jam out Beatles' tunes and other classic rock.

Lighting is not limited to just musical programming either. Christmas lights, colored bulbs, and backlights can create a mood to suit any program. A book discussion club talking about murder mysteries and forensic sciences could meet under UV lights. A science-based program could feature astronomical projections on the ceiling.

The floors can be a great place to hide information. Measure out the room in arcane units like cubits, or give size references in relation to geological or cosmological bodies. For example, how many libraries can fit inside the sun?

A blast from the classroom past, the overhead projector can be a fantastic tool for filling up the walls of a huge space. Playing classic party games like Pictionary™ or charades with an overhead projector as part of the mix gives a whole new spin on the classics. Projectors can also be used as a basic camera obscura, casting a traceable shape on the large sheets of paper hung from the walls.

Use the large walls to your every advantage. Posting up butcher paper can create an instant art zone on every wall that that can be moved and leaves no mess behind. Think big with wall-sized mural projects. Invite teens to design a green city, and then draw the plan on the walls. Use papered walls like chalkboard; encourage teens to write their thoughts on the walls during discussions. Create an on-going poetry jam wall that's added to weekly. Or play a long-term game of exquisite corpse, in which each participant adds a line to the story. How about creating an endless comic book or tapestry telling the history of your community or simply the lives of the teenagers in it? All of this encourages teenagers to feel comfortable in a space, bend some of the usual social conventions, and express themselves in open, safe, and fun ways.

Ancient humans first huddled in caves for warmth and company. It was only when they started drawing on the walls that those caves became home.

THE HOBBIT HOLE

The fantasist author J.R.R. Tolkien said that his inspiration for the massive cycle that would one day encompass *The Lord of the Rings* saga came from the simple sentence: "There once was a hobbit who lived in a hole." Though Tolkien's hobbits lived in holes, they were a fastidious people whose penchant for making the very best of their limited living space was a matter of no small pride. There's nothing wrong with making a nook or a cranny home: there's even literary precedent for it.

Sometimes, the only spaces available for use as programming spaces are not exactly on the large side of things. Older library buildings might have a plethora of silent study spaces, but a real lack of communal space. In part, this reflects the (positive) changes in the role of the library. Rather than a place for simple quiet study, libraries are now vibrant community spaces.

In some cases libraries cannot expand for monetary reasons, or perhaps community space is at a premium, or perhaps the planning of the library space did not take into account the need for a communal programming space that would accessible to youth programming. As an aside, these kinds of issues are why librarians unique skill set and understanding of just what kind of services the library offers on a regular basis are vital to any expansion or building that goes on in and for a library. It's a sad fact that too many times librarians find themselves dealing with a construction project that does not address the daily realities of library programming. As one librarian put it at an American Library Association (ALA) conference I attended a number of years ago: "If you have to sneak into the architect's office, do it!"

Beyond agitating for the great glory of the Master's degree in library science (MLS), there does come a moment when you might have to just accept having limited space to work with. Perhaps you can only use two, oddly shaped study rooms. Perhaps you have a large meeting room, but the tables and chairs are bolted to the floor (this is an odd design choice that seems to have found some adherents in the 1960s and 1970s) thus limiting what can be done with the space. Perhaps your only communal space is also the story time/playroom, which features permanent "little kid" decorations, stuffed animals, and no real options for seating. Let's deal with each of these in turn.

DO MORE WITH LESS

Study rooms are sometimes the only communal space in a youth services department that is not dedicated to much younger patrons. These spaces are excellent for study groups and young people just looking for a place to read and chat that isn't too silent. Making use of these study room spaces as community gathering spaces may seem like an odd idea at first, but they can in fact play out as fun and flexible spaces.

Most study rooms feature some kind of clear glass wall or partition as a safety measure. Think of this glass as a large-scale artistic space. Turn the glass walls into stained-glass windows, add color and light with painting projects, give the windows a dramatic style. By laying out sheeting to keep the floors clean, you can allow young adults to paint in groups and shifts.

Study rooms are also useful for more sedate activities, such as board game tournaments, table-top role-playing, and arts and craft projects. One advantage to a smaller space is the ability to do more involved programming with a smaller group. Teaching origami, knitting, or box making can be complex, especially for beginners. A smaller "classroom" can help a great deal.

Food and drink in programming is always a challenge. The mess and clean up is often used as a reason for avoiding them altogether. A smaller space allows more control over the materials as well as a smaller batch of "cooks." One successful program I ran was teaching how to create vegetarian sushi. I had run the program in a large conference room to an audience of nearly 30. It was hectic and fun, but I felt some of the finer details about Japanese culture and cooking was lost in all the frenetic fun of rolling up maki. When I ran the program in a much smaller space with just a handful of young adult patrons, there was a great deal more discussion and the program spiked a real interest in culture programming.

One more advantage of a study room space is how they lend themselves to more open conversations. While a popular series of books might draw a large crowd, more challenging reading, perhaps dealing with more serious subject matter, draws a smaller crowd. I've run several book discussions for the memoir *A Child Called It*, which is a perennial favorite for getting "lost" at every library I've worked at in my career. The book's intense descriptions of serious child abuse strikes a chord with many kids. Sometimes this is a matter of burgeoning empathy, and sometimes it's a young person finding a common voice for his or her own struggles. In more than one discussion I've spoken with young people who were inspired by the story, concerned for a friend, or even expressing their own worries about emotional issues at home. A smaller space can let a young person feel at ease in discussing weighty issues.

THE SEATS DON'T MOVE

Permanent furniture is, hopefully, one tragedy of the 20th century that we can leave in that all too unkind century. Desks bolted to floors, chairs bolted to walls, and my favorite, the heavy chair. The Heavy Chair, which I have capitalized as a proper noun for all its ugly glory, is any seating that exceeds the weight and mass of a sumo wrestler and is, ostensibly, used for seating. These enormous seats are, technically, moveable, but are often so far beyond the ability of even the most toned librarian to move that they may as well not be. I've watched a whole department of healthy, in-shape librarians line up to move a Heavy Chair like medieval peasants trying to pull Excalibur from the stone. Not a one of them was Arthur.

So what do you do when facing down a room that was designed with all the malleability of a stage set for an episode of *The Tomorrow Show* with Tom Snyder circa 1976? Seats that won't move, tables that are bulky and staid, no room to give? The challenge here is to think around the problem, and in a sense, around the furniture.

As mentioned before, creating a focal point for your programming is important. Fixed furniture is often centered on a focal point. Whether that is a dais, a podium, or just the front of the room, you have a natural place to stand and present. Fixed seating may limit where your audience can move, but that's an advantage if you're willing to develop a sense of play. Create "assigned seating" for events. You could even create tickets for film screenings or presenters. This lends an air of formality as well as serves the ever-present need to compile good and solid statistics.

Play with the space as much as you can. If you're running a book discussion, one with a lighter tone, you can hide questions or topics under various seats. Put them towards the back to draw in more shy participants. Another similar use is placing prizes or treats for any number of programs somewhere on the fixed furniture. It's a bit of a lift from *Oprah* but surprise is always a great way of getting attention with young adults.

Most critical of all, acknowledge the limitations of that space. Be aware but know that your audience is aware as well. Be open to suggestions ,and most of all, let young adults define their own space as well. Maybe they all want to grab a seat on the floor in a semi-circle, maybe they want to sit in formal rows, or cluster in odd little groups. Let them find their equilibrium, and you'll have more energy to focus on the program at hand.

THE FLUFFY BUNNY TEENAGER ROOM

As I've said before, nothing drives a teenager further away than accusing them of being a child. The modem concept of teenagers and young adults is one that some communities, and by extension, their libraries wrestle with. So you find that the "kids" room is meant to house everything from "Lapsit with Mommy and Daddy" to "How to Plan Your College Trip."

There are moments as a librarian that one feels as if Lewis Carroll is not only alive, but somehow the author of your fate. Sitting at a tiny table that could very well serve as a scale model of a tiny table for very small children while discussing the visceral horror of Stephen King's It with a group of bemused high school students certainly put me in mind of a certain kind of tea party.

Sometimes the only option available to you as a young adult librarian is to use a space that is not built to your age specifications. A room filled with charming stuffed animals and cute murals might work wonders for the smaller set, but it can really put off young adults.

It might sound like a trivial complaint, but bear in mind that in their attempts to self-define as neither young children or adults, every little bit helps, or hurts. Making a room that feels fit for safety scissors and picture books a home for the young adult manga club or Guitar Hero Championships is an awkward fit.

The first step is assessing what you can simply put out of sight, and thus, out of mind. If you're able to make use of a closet or storage area try gathering up toys and stuffed animals. It's not to say that you have to create a space that feels austere or ever cold. This author will confess to owning a shelf full of stuffies including "My little Cthulhu," a stuffed bat, and a panda fox. Striking the balance between what will be curious and fun to young adults and what might make them feel they're in a space meant for much younger patrons is a bit of a challenge.

Lighting is a cheap and easy way to change a room's character. I previously mentioned black lights, Christmas lighting, and colored gels. Even track and spot lighting can help give a room a completely different feel. Spaces for very young children are often extremely brightly lit. Even just dimming the light levels, brings the room in a bit and can make a huge difference.

Again, creating a focal point is key. If you are giving a scientific program creating banners and signs that direct attention away from decorations and on to your presentation not only help maintain attention, they can make the room feel custom built for your program.

AND THE CROWD GOES WILD

More and more, libraries are serving the role of "third space" in communities. In times of economic turmoil, families can turn to libraries as an alternative to the more expensive forms of entertainment and "edutainment" found elsewhere. Libraries can best deal with this increase in demand by expanding and experimenting with programming and programming spaces. After all, a larger audience means a wider base of patrons with diverse interests and needs. Looking upon a growing patron base as an opportunity to find new uses for library spaces is a way of turning a challenge into an expansion.

It almost goes without saying that talking to young adults about what they like and dislike about the space is important. This goes double when talking about spaces for programming. Young adults interest in programming can be deeply impacted by the space, in some ways more so than adults. Small children generally tuck in, only off-put by discomfort or stress, and adults are generally able to make allowances, but teenagers often require a bit more attention to detail to keep their focus.

It's worth noting that the much ballyhooed drop-off of teenage interest in libraries and programming may be due, in no small part, to a lack of dedicated programming spaces for teens as much as any other factor. As a rule, the whole argument feels cyclical really; with the assumption that teens are a lost cause feeding the notion that creating a space for them is a waste of time, which leads to fewer young adults coming in.

The take away is that creating and adapting spaces, big, small, and in between for challenging and creative young adult programming is something any librarian can accomplish, and the benefits, especially in creating lifelong library loving patrons, are simply too good to pass up.

5

◆ ◆ ◆

STEREOTYPES THAT BIND

HANGING WITH THE BREAKFAST CLUB

In the 1980s a writer and director named John Hughes defined American youth culture for a generation. With films like *Ferris Bueller's Day Off,* *Pretty in Pink,* and *Sixteen Candles,* Hughes spoke to young adults with frankness about love and identity in a way that few filmmakers had done before. It's why, even though the teens he was writing for now have children and even teenagers of their own, his films still strike a resonant chord with teenagers. One film in particular, *The Breakfast Club,* has become nothing short of a classic for teenagers since its release.

The film's premise is simple. A grab bag of teenagers are thrown together for weekend detention. Each of them represents a stereotypical teenager. The "Princess" and the "Athlete" represent the upper echelon of high school society. The "Brain" is the nerd, whose intelligence isolates him and breeds resentment. The "Basket Case" spends her time in a world of her own creation, and finally, the " Criminal" challenges all of them while he suffers deeply.

These young people are thrown together in, of all places, a library. Most of the film concerns itself with how these young people see each other and how they really see themselves. It's a pop culture spin on dramatic classics like *No Exit* or even *The Decameron*. It is, without sounding too windy on the subject, what William Faulkner meant when he spoke of great art as being "the human heart in conflict with itself."

It's also one of the most valuable films for any professional who works with young adults to have seen at least a half-dozen times.

The underlying message of the film is that while these characters are as they appear on the surface, they are also shades of every other stereotype. Every saint is a sinner, every jock, a nerd. No teenager is simple.

A fine piece of homespun wisdom that I've hewn to is that there are no "bad kids." That every young adult is going to have good and bad days, hours, even moments. Beyond the simple madness of puberty and physical development that drives them to distraction with all its myriad vicissitudes, there is the simple fact that teenagers are often in the business of trying on rebellion the way an adult would try on clothes. Personas are fluid, mercurial even, and where one day you are presented with a sharp-tongued rapscallion with nothing but the worst to hiss at you over some arbitrary policy, the next day you might have, in the same young person, an adroit and kindly assistant. Patience and persistence leads the way.

But planning programming on moods, building a space based on the shifting temperaments of young people, is a challenge to even the most patient librarian.

In this chapter, I'll be taking some of the most hoary stereotypes and using them as a filter, a means of looking at and addressing the patron needs of young adults passing through these phases, trying on these personas. By no means do these stereotypes encompass the whole of young adult personalities, not by a long shot. Rather these serve as a gateway, a lens, a camera obscura for viewing patrons who are still trying to see themselves clearly.

NERDS: NO NEED FOR REVENGE

Even writing the word *nerd* can cause a flinch. It's an invective, an insult, and a cruel slur. A term that brings to mind social awkwardness, lack of personal style, and a sort of creeping discomfort with the word. Nerds are fascinated with ephemera and trivia. They might recite to you the "Encounter Table" odds for a table-top role-playing game or random facts about the development of the *Hitchhiker's Guide to the Galaxy Universe*. Nerds are not cool; they're the antithesis of cool. Call them geeks, dorks, spazzes, Trekkies, or just plain old nerds: none of the terms are very kind.

It has been observed that the computer revolution of the late 20th century is nothing short of the greatest comeuppance so-called nerds could ever hope for. Suddenly the world was suffused with technology that has, with stunning alacrity, overtaken the general public's ability to comprehend it.

Here is a bit of a thought experiment to give a sense of just how vital the nerd has become in every day life. A home in mid-century America might contain a few specialized pieces of technology, but not too many. A water heater, a furnace, a washer and dryer, items that worked on generally understood principles. Natural gas was not all that different from other forms of heat. Television and radio were complex, but again they functioned on practical principles, antennae and waves on the air to be received.

Then comes the home computer, a device that promises to revolutionize work and create whole new avenues of play and creative endeavor. The first computers came in kits; only those who understood them could build them. But soon enough, the layperson was working desktop, often with almost no idea how the device actually did what it was doing. When something went wrong, there was suddenly little recourse. How do you fix something you barely understand? It's a trend that continues into the 21st century, where phones and tiny portable computers function at levels of technological development that they might as well be magical, even to an educated person.

But not to a nerd.

Cool has been redefined. Yes, the billionaires of Silicon Valley are uniformly nerds. The Internet, before it was flooded with everyone, was built and pioneered by nerds. Nerds craft spectacles of modern special effects. Scientist heroes on the forefront of every major breakthrough are, yes, nerds. The same joyous obsessions that cost them dearly as young people have made them into great minds.

I had an art teacher once who made the grandiose statement that artists need not suffer to be great. She claimed that the noble, pained creator, the tragic clown, the heartbreak that drives the genius, that all that was fantasy. She herself was an artist, and she was quite content. I was part of a contingent who argued against her on this point (citing everyone from Van Gogh to Dorothy Parker to Hemingway) but she persisted. The final day of class she brought in some of her art. Tacky plastic bracelets, huge and bulky and so carelessly put together that two of them broke as she showcased them.

Nerds understand suffering. Whether it comes from an overemphasis on mental activity, no physical development or a simple lack of understanding when it comes to some of the more blatant social cues in schooling, nerds often find themselves alone with their thoughts and obsessions. Great artists are nerds as much as great programmers. Really, being a nerd is being passionate about something past the point of worrying what others think of your passion.

Societies as a whole often accept nerds in certain contexts. Doctors, lawyers, financers, all toil away for years on minutiae that would make the average person's eyes cross. But they're held in high esteem, pinnacles of achievement. But then, everything changed.

Again, the seismic shift, the winning of the culture war by the nerd class, shines through. The creep of high-end technology into every facet of life has opened up whole new vistas for those with busy minds dedicated to obscure arts.

It seems almost obvious that nerds can be found in the library. Every youth librarian has stories about wonderful and charming young people who are delightfully geeky. The young man building a model rocket, the young girl running a months-long live-action role-playing game, the gaggle of gamers who can't wait to regale you with stories of their latest exploits deep in the heart of some massive multiplayer online game— nerds abound in the library.

Keeping all that in mind, how do you make room for nerds in your library? The answer is simple: stand back, hold fast, and give in.

Appealing to intellectually minded teens means allowing them to follow their interests. If their obsession is with the western comic media this month you're not going to snag them by running an anime series. But if you open up and say you're open to all kinds of graphic literature, you can let them define the specifics, which they assuredly will.

Again, it's finding the balance between openness and order. When trying to define a space, the more flexibility you can build in the better. Computer stations that don't allow for collaboration feel closed. Nerds like openness, inquiry, and exploration. It may seem odd, but the most likely young person to challenge a seemingly arbitrary policy is likely quite nerdy in their own right. Policies and practices that don't have solid intellectual footing are fresh meat for the young intellectual, a call to arms. So locking away the computer room at 5 P.M. on the dot simply because that's how it's always been is likely to raise a challenge.

Noticing an emphasis on technological activities? True to form, a nerd is going to want to get their hands on the tech. We'll talk about technology in a general sense in a later chapter, but when dealing with nerds, the goal is to keep things as open as possible.

This begins with computers but can extend to nearly any library technology. A self-checkout can sometimes stymie older and less tech-savvy patrons. Deputizing your frequent young adult nerdy patrons on the machines is one way to build a knowledge base quickly and spread support for the new system.

Books on audio file and e-readers are more and more commonplace. Creating a reading nook especially for using these burgeoning technologies is one way to promote them to nerds and beyond. Set up a "Kindle Corner" (or if you must be corny "Kindle *Korner*") that features not just the readers but also handy explanations of how they work and related library policies.

Let nerds get their hands on tech and science but don't neglect the humanities either. Tapping into the interests of drama students, costume designers. and artists of all kinds is invaluable when decorating a space, developing a program, or simply looking to develop the collection to best suit their ever-shifting tastes.

Because libraries are places that exhaust learning, the attraction is obvious. We librarians ourselves are the very apotheosis of the nerd. We devote our lives to the systemization, categorization, and dissemination of knowledge from every culture in the world. It wouldn't be unfair or the least bit unkind to call us "über-nerds."

FEAR OF JOCKS

Perhaps it is the somewhat nerdy origins of many a librarian that leads to so much misunderstanding when it comes to jocks. First, lets talk about the term itself. The connection to athletic supporters, the guttural sound, it's all about diminishing the intelligence of the individual. Jocks are considered to be lunkheads. Think of *Back to the Future* where the bad guy, a jock thug named Biff, has the oh so clever line: "Hey, make like a tree . . . and get out of here." Jocks represent the ascent of brawn over brains. Call them sportos, meatheads, tuffs, or muscle heads, the idea is the same.

I won't be so naive as to argue that jocks are blameless. Many school social hierarchies place an enormous emphasis on sports and those who play them. American society salaries that would shame pharaohs go to a tiny cadre of athletic elites. The most well-paid teacher (or librarian) would be a pauper in the ranks of the NFL or NBA.

Athletic accomplishments are more immediate in a sense. Progress in a sport is easier to track than in the study of a field or one's development as an artist. Win the meet, score the goal, beat the record: a more clearly defined vision of success is possible with sports.

That kind of linear progression isn't necessarily antithetical to an enjoyable library experience. After all, libraries are all about the progress of knowledge, connecting patron and materials in a way that is not dissimilar from any kind of physical development.

But the library can be so . . . quiet.

Spend any time on a court, field, or pitch, and you'll find that it's noisy. Jocks are exuberant; from the clichéd roar of the crowd to trash talk to the simple sounds of athletes make when working their bodies without even thinking about it. Tennis pros often make hellacious noise when going up for a serve, somewhere between a scream and grunt.

We can trace this tendency to make noise back to the primitive nature of competition. If you're not very big, make a big noise. And if you are big, make an even bigger noise. Claim the very air around you. There's a catharsis to the freedom of noise in sport.

But the library . . . the library is so very . . . quiet.

Loath as I am to use ellipses, they fit here so very well. Because there is that awkward pause when jocks enter the library, rolling in from practice or just having a run and then suddenly . . . the hush of the library.

Of course, modern libraries have been shaking off the tiresome tomb images for years now, but there's still a feeling of hush, quiet, and "insideness" that rolls over the patrons. For jocks, being quiet is an anathema.

Drawing jocks into the library is in part overcoming the age-old perception of the library as a place where physicality and boisterousness are not only not welcome, but subjects of scorn. The sad old visage of a librarian looking down her nose and spectacles at some rabble-rousers is deeply ingrained.

Designing spaces that appeal to jocks is relatively easy. Jocks like to crash; they like to just drop in, take a knee, and find a place to stretch out a bit. Having a part of your teen space with big cushy chair, even something low and on the floor to drop down on would do wonders to attract jocks. Don't sweat the delicates; emphasize physical comfort and the ability to stretch out. Again, it's a question of body awareness. A jock who puts their feet up and slouches down is still reading and enjoying the library as much as the teen with great posture using the furniture "correctly."

What about noise? While the trend to more friendly and open library spaces is a good one to pursue generally, there are some steps to take in the day to day. If possible, create a "loud space" in your library. Whether it's a designated study room with good sound-proofing or a section of the story room that gets shut off for part of the day, create a space where jocks can blast some of the music in the collection, watch a movie, or simply laugh and hang out loud and proud.

Adding programming that incorporates physicality is also a great draw. Book-truck races and scavenger hunts can get the blood pumping. After-hours lock-ins where library space is repurposed as a play area (with good and proper supervision) can instill a lifelong appreciation for the possibilities of what a jock can do in the library. Much better they remember having fun in the library than worrying about what they'll be told they cannot do by the ghost of librarians long since passed.

BUT I'M A CHEERLEADER

Thus far in examining these stereotypes, I've steered as clear as I can away from gender profiling. A girl's lacrosse team once did more damage to a library I worked in than a group of boys three times their size. At first look the "Cheerleader" or "Prom Queen" might seem like a very unenlightened way to talk about young women. The stereotype we're talking about here isn't exclusively female, not at all. We're talking about the connector, the social teenager who has developed a network of friends and acquaintances. We could call this young person a social director or simply, a social butterfly.

These teens are often the arbiters of taste and style in their social groups, and even beyond. They define what and who is and is not cool and often are surrounded by hangers-on who ape their style. The Prom Queen is the epitome of the modern wired (or wireless) teenager. Phones, most likely smartphone with text, SMS, and online capabilities, are as essential to these teenagers as their backpacks.

These teens travel in groups, almost exclusively. Watching a group of these young people move from table to table, from study area to study area, almost bird-like in their flocking behavior can be fascinating. Their conversations move with a speed that would likely flummox their parent's generation. The technology that binds them adds a silent level of communication, both text and picture messages further complicate matters for the older set looking on.

In 2001, when I first began to work in libraries as a grad student, the standing policy towards cell phones was an absolute ban on their use in the library. By the time I was working as a librarian, that policy had softened to allow for cell phone use that was not disruptive. Now it's mainly corralling people who tend to think that the smaller the phone the louder they must yell out of the stacks.

The Prom Queen's use of a cell phone is as a primary communication and coordination device. It's a catalog of photos; it connects to their online "digital shadow" (a concept we'll get more into in the next chapter); and, put simply, it runs their life. The concept that a cell phone is anything short of a basic necessity (or more controversially amongst parents, a "right") is simply an alien concept.

Lest you think this assessment speaks only of teens from more affluent communities, it's worth noting that cell phones market saturation on a yearly basis far exceeds the number of teen purchasers and is only climbing. In a world where an iPhone™ can be gotten for under a hundred dollars, every phone is a smartphone accessible to all.

The image presented thus far is not exactly one that seems in line with a comfortable fit for the library. A great deal of talking, reliance on technology for ephemera, social/reputation-based economy, how can all this work in making room at the library for the Prom Queen?

Create chat spaces. Like the noisy rumpus room for the jocks, have a dedicated space or place where conversation can get a little loud and a little goofy.

Using phones and social networking to advertise is a given, but developing spaces that are alive on the Internet is even more effective. The advent of micro-blogging sites like Twitter (which allow users to upload up to 140 characters of text that can then be "followed" by anyone) mean that communication takes on another, even more meta level. Why not have "tweeting" spaces in the library? What if your designated teen/young adult space itself had a Twitter account? Broadcasting not just events coming up, but events right then and there?

One nagging question is that of efficacy when it comes to these kinds of digital endeavors. Building a Web site that no one reads or posting updates online that no one sees is just a fool's errand. One way of testing the audience is arranging a contest that is listed exclusively online. Post a blog entry that says the first five patrons to check out a graphic novel and use the phrase "The Dark Knight Returns" will receive movie passes. Make these contests or games a regular feature in a medium that feels most natural to young adults like the prom queen.

Like the jock, it's always a sound idea to simply step back and let the socializing and simple hanging out take place. Not being hung-up on hard and fast rules about how many teens can sit at a table or use a computer or use a study room are slight but effective ways of communicating that you understand the importance of socializing and talking with friends. It makes the space and the library as a whole feel more approachable to these social butterflies when they choose to light.

WEIRD TALES

I freely confess I was a weird teenager. Growing up in the mid to late 1990s, I was given to 10-eye green Doc Marten boots, fedoras, and long duster coats. I could often be found in my high school library, bent over books by Harlan Ellison, Neil Gaiman, and Vladimir Nabokov. I was set to fume about any of the world's many injustices and often found myself battering away with teachers and classmates alike.

I was pretty tedious and about 10 kinds of weird.

Weirdoes have perhaps the toughest row to hoe of any of our token stereotypes. They choose a life less ordinary in many respects. Marching to the beat of your own drummer when conformity is abundant takes a bit of steel in the backbone.

Weirdoes, outliers, outsiders, freaks, and creeps are all words that can hurt even years after the fact. Nothing damages a teenager as much as feeling that they are not welcome. While some choose to keep their own council, many more would simply like to pass invisibly into their college years and beyond. In some ways, they've accepted that adolescence is not a time they're going to enjoy and they believe they will be better off when it's over. It can be difficult for a young adult librarian to hear this, especially since many of us, at heart, still hold onto a part of our teenage years. It's a bit of the fuel that drives us.

Weirdoes haven't had an easy time of it in recent years because of the perception that outsiders are "dangerous," perhaps even prone to school violence. The kid listening to Swedish death metal with the big scary boots and long shaggy hair seems to many a great deal more worrisome than Joe Popular.

Incidents of school violence are committed by students from diverse backgrounds and social groups. Marginalizing or branding a student already on the periphery of his social groups as a possible threat serves little purpose.

Most weirdoes are simply not focused on the trials and tribulations of high school social dynamics. Perhaps they are focused on their art. Perhaps they are independent learners who look forward to college. Perhaps they're writers or filmmakers who aren't finding much support in their home or school life. Whatever the case, weirdoes are still as passionate and excited as any young adult, even if their means of expression is a bit different from the norm.

Drawing in weirdoes to the library isn't that difficult. Libraries offer a refuge for freethinkers of all kinds. Whether it's a passion for science fiction or military history or indie music, weirdoes can find something in the library that meets their interest with a level gaze. Building library spaces to accommodate these outliers is more of a challenge.

One aspect of being on the outside looking in is that, on some level, you relish the difference between yourself and others. This is not to say that every outsider is looking down with a haughty gaze upon the world. Rather it's a question of feeling comfortable in your own skin, far removed from the pressing concerns of other social cliques and groups. How to build a space around a young person who is, in some ways, looking for an escape from the community is a tough quandary to tackle.

One tactic is to build in spaces that are unique and a bit removed. A chair set off to the side or risers that are a bit boxed offers a sort of mini refuge. This is not to say that the space should be inaccessible, but much like the forts small children (and some adults) build out of sofa cushions and pillows, it offers a bit of refuge in plain sight.

If study rooms can be spared, consider making one into a cloistered reading space. Somewhere that feels tucked away and yet not so far off the beaten path that the young adult feels left out.

Can these outsiders be a powerful form of outreach? While electronic communication and school postings might reach many, many weirdoes might not be reached. Like the other stereotypes addressed, these young adults share information in their own circles at their own pace. Consider the fact that reaching out to a single outlier could serve as a form of outreach to a whole community of youth who might otherwise be difficult tap. Outsiders can often be powerful agents of outreach and vocal supporters of libraries. In some respects, their endorsement of a program or a space carries more weight than most, as they are not know for being overly effusive.

One point worth keeping at the front of your mind when considering how to reach out to these sometimes difficult teens, is just how much it means to be acknowledged for who you are and what you're doing. That sounds Pollyanna perhaps, but in truth being acknowledged for who they really are is what weirdoes deeply long for from adults. They want to know that you think their peculiar demeanor is ok, that they can be themselves, and that you will not try to harass back into a more traditional vision of adolescence. Say you see a young adult matching this particular stereotype curled up, feet on the armrest, reading contentedly. Sure, you could invite them to the program running in the teen area, put on the hard sell, and hope they can be won over. Or you could simply let them know they're welcome but that what they're up to, or not up to, is fine all the same.

When you've been the square peg, there's nothing more frustrating than yet another person trying to shove you in triangle-shaped hole.

THE STEREOTYPE IS VAST AND CONTAINS MULTITUDES

As you may have already guessed, there's a great deal of overlap in these stereotypical young adults and in the approaches to working with them in a library space. In part, this comes from the somewhat basic universality of good practices and open communication. Establishing good relationships with teens, regardless of their general disposition or clique, is part and parcel of being a good young adult librarian.

But there is a bigger issue here, which is that every young adult is capable of moving through any flimsy definition on a daily basis. The Jock whose weight-training and fitness regime is based on very nerdy scientific principle. The Prom Queen whose entire persona exists online and is in person quite a shy and quiet weirdo. The Weirdo who finds theater and ends up a social superstar. Adolescence is a time to be who you think you might be, even if only for a day. It's the challenge of young adult librarians to develop spaces, programming, and outreach that not only grasps the most transient of personality shifts, but also embraces the whole spectrum. The library should be a place where any teenager can feel welcome at any time.

Again, thinking of teenagers in broad, often silly, stereotypes is not something I'd recommend as a sound planning stratagem. But at the same time, looking at the various moods and "phases" that any given teen might embrace at any given moment helps those of us whose teen years are far behind us to understand these shifting patrons better.

The Breakfast Club ends with the students writing a triumphant letter to the overbearing principal. The students, having formed bonds far beyond their comfort zones and having challenged each other to accept the multitudes they each contain, write that they are each a brain, an athlete, a princess, a criminal, and a basket case. As the "criminal" of the group makes his way home, he raises a triumphant fist on the football field. While this might sound like 1980s nostalgia, it is, in fact, a statement of the power of looking beyond stereotypes, embracing our multifaceted natures and being all the stronger for it.

6

◇ ◇ ◇

TECHNOBABBLE

DIGITAL KILLED THE ANALOG STAR

I was most fortunate in library school to be taught by an instructor who recalled some of the very first "dumb terminals" being installed back in the early 1980s. This was at a prestigious, one might even say "ivy-covered," university, and my instructor was a fresh young librarian eager to embrace the new technology.

Of course, the professors were lining up with pitchforks and torches demanding that the "damnable robot libraries" be smashed into flinders. Once the flinders were buried, the ground could be salted, and the land left to lie fallow for a number of generations.

And that was the moderate opinion.

Technology has never been a runaway hit in libraries. Every hiccup of the electronic catalog would cause librarians of an older generation to roll their eyes and tut-tut about the simplicity of the card catalog. Every new feature that ended up causing a new bug would be sighed over. Any patron incapable of embracing the organization and systemization of knowledge unique to the bibliographic arts was lamented as one more Gaul with a spear at the gates of Rome. Technology as advancement towards ruin.

Part of this is generational. This is not to speak broadly of any one generation, that's folly and leaves no room for the millions of outliers, but there is something to be said for those born "digital native" versus those coming to computers later in life.

As a child of the late 1980s and early 1990s, I lived a life suffused with technology. Whether it was games like "Oregon Trail" at school or swapping out CD-ROMs on early PC games at home, computers were front and center in my life. When I entered high school, my graduating class was actually the last to learn typing on typewriters, and even that was due to a lag in building a proper computer lab.

It wasn't just computers either. Technology pervaded every aspect of my generation's life. From the rise of the Internet, online communication and telecommunications all became part and parcel of being a young adult by the end of the 1990s.

The generation before us? They might look at the previous two paragraphs the same way I might look at the reminisces of a telegraph operator from the old west.

"WATSON, COME IN HERE, I TEXTED YOU"

I had a pager in 1998. This was a big deal, as my family thought pagers were only for medical doctors and drug dealers. Since I was a history major at the time and not a drug dealer, the purchase was met with some suspicion.

I tried explaining the concept of a pager to a young adult recently, and was met with nothing short of a blank gaze.

"So, people could call you, but you had to get another phone to call them back?"

"Yes."

"That's stupid."

"No, see, if people needed me, I would know."

"But what if you couldn't find a phone."

"Erm. Well. Then you couldn't respond."

"See? Stupid."

My cool, hip, non-drug dealing/non-medical student self in 1998 would have been mortified.

This young adult I spoke with has a phone, and not just any phone, but an iPhone. A brand so ubiquitous and known that it almost seems silly to explain that an iPhone is a smartphone made by Apple that is capable of serving as both a phone and Internet platform. It's a device that, in the few short years since its launch, has completely dominated the market and defined, in essence, what that market is to the consumer. Whenever a new and shinier bauble comes rolling along, it is questioned whether this device will be the lauded "iPhone Killer." As if the iPhone were some lycanthrope, a werewolf haunting the fog-shrouded woods, waiting for a brave hunter to come put it down.

Teenagers today live at tech speed. It's not a matter of "if" they have a phone but "when" and "what kind." The proliferation of communications technology is spread from one end of the socioeconomic spectrum to the other. We'll discuss later how the digital divide is still pressing issue but without a doubt the past decade has seen that gap narrow in the most unexpected ways.

THE IT CROWD

The misuse of the word *evolution* in reference to technological advancement is a bugbear of mine. Evolution is the slow, gradual process of change over time. It's a process of millions of years that involves the wear and tear of centuries of environmental adaptation. Technology, especially information technology, is more like the grade-school science class observation of fruit fly mutation. Perhaps you recall this exercise. Fruit flies breed so rapidly that mutations in their genetic code are visible within a single generation. It's evolution in microcosm, sans environmental factors. Mutants in a bubble. That's a pretty apt description of most IT departments. (That is, of course, a loving joke. Please don't make my computer explode.)

Librarians are information scientists. Focusing on the systemization and cataloging of knowledge is no less a scientific endeavor than counting stars or tracking pathogens. There are standards of intellect and rigor to which we, as librarians, adhere. Yet many librarians are not computer scientists, nor are they programmers or technicians. While many librarians are versed as so-called end-users of technology, there is still little in the way of requirement for librarians to be more than minimally computer proficient. This leaves many libraries at the whim of IT professionals.

My first position in a library was working as a middleman between librarians and the IT professionals at the library. I thought of myself as a sort of IT EMT, trying to keep the patient (in this case, the computer) alive until such time as a trained computer professional could do more detailed work. Often this was little more than turning the machine off and on again.

The IT department viewed the patrons in much the same way as the Roman Empire viewed the Visigoths. From them I would often be asked questions like:

"Can't you keep them from *banging* on the keyboards?"

"How the hell does someone get gum *behind* the screen of a monitor?"

"There is a . . . substance . . . in this fan vent. I don't think it's from nature. What happened?"

The librarians often framed their tech questions in purposefully vague terms. As if ignorance of technology was some manner of forbearance against its inexorable march.

"I don't know. It's a disk, thingee. To get online. For the Internet."

"The Internet logged off again. No, I don't know how."

"This game is stuck. I don't know the rules so I left it."

I present these ancient quotes from the dawn of the 21st century not just for their comic value but to give a sense of the digital divide—the divide between librarians and the technology that suffuses our profession—that often goes unnoticed in libraries.

THE END USER AND YOU

How does your cell phone work? Can you explain how the touch screen of a smartphone operates? How does upgrading RAM change the power of a computer? What's the difference between Wi-Fi™ and Bluetooth™?

On the surface, these are simple questions. The kind of reference questions librarians face every day. But can you really give more than a superficial answer to any of them without significant technical expertise? You might be able to explain cell towers and signal strength, but the hardware and software that make those things happen are complex. You can set up your home Wi-Fi, perhaps with more ease than setting the clock on a VCR, but the technology in the box and on your computer that drive the signal are beyond most end users.

That's what technology has accomplished for us, or done to us, depending on your point of view. We live in a time when communication is easier, information is more accessible, and human beings are better informed than any time in history. Yet the technology that drives this might as well be the stuff of sorcery.

The famed writer Arthur C. Clarke once remarked, "Any sufficiently advanced technology is indistinguishable from magic." It's worth noting that Clarke knew of what he spoke not just as an author, but as a technologist as well. He was the first to propose the modern communications satellite, the invention that got modern global communications rolling.

As librarians we use technology on a daily basis that, even a decade ago, was the stuff of science fiction. Handheld computing, massive data storage, and telecommunication have opened up the world. Yet that technology often feels daunting, even alien, to many librarians.

Young adults intuitive understanding of technology is the butt of every lazy comedian's joke. Need your computer fixed? Ask an eight-year-old. The digital natives born in the 1980s and after see computers as something that can be fitted and adjusted to their needs. They swim in a sea of information and seem to, almost intuitively, adapt to changes that often stymie adults.

How then can we, as those stymied adults, best create technological spaces in libraries to appeal to an audience that is, in many ways, hipper than us? It's not a simple answer, but like any other aspect of library design, it's a question of understanding the needs of the patron first.

FILTERING: A HEADY BREW

Nothing can fill a librarian with more joy than seeing row after row of happy young adults, busily typing away the afternoon. Are they knee-deep?

No, they're playing RuneScape™.

Or they're playing the latest game on Facebook, or using any number of social networking sites to upload pictures, gossip, tweet, and connect. By the time this book goes to press a half-dozen new sites and services will have already risen to the heights of cool and plummeted out of favor.

Whatever they're doing on those Internet terminals, they are most certainly not sticking to the handcrafted Web guide provided by hardworking librarians.

And there is nothing wrong with that. Really.

The notion that all young adult use of library computers must be strictly homework related is not only unrealistic, it's punitive. Libraries are about providing access, not making sure that every technological experience is somehow an educational one.

The issue that comes up of course is that of "inappropriate material." Internet filtering software has been ongoing within the library community for years. The debate about its effectiveness has raged across librarian e-mail lists and forums, and in conference halls (long before librarians started using e-mail lists), and shows little sign of abating. The debate came to a head with the passage of CIPA (Children's Internet Protection Act), a federal law that took effect in 2004. CIPA mandates that any library that accepts federal funds for computers with Internet access is required to place filtering software on their computers.

While this did not apply to all libraries, state governments enacted similar provisions across the country. By 2005, over 65 percent of public libraries had some or all of their Internet–accessing computers filtered. While the efficacy of that filtering is a matter still hotly debated, the reality for many libraries is that filters were a part of daily life.

But filtering out sexual and violent content (as well as, some would argue perfectly harmless or even useful information) is just one aspect of monitoring Internet usage. Again, how to best define what is and is not an "appropriate" use of library computers? This is an instance where designing a space for teenagers can help to deal with a thorny issue.

OVERSEEING, NOT OVERBEARING

The best way to make a kid a crook is to treat them like one. The assumption that young adults are constantly up to no good is one that leads to more friction than simply giving teenagers the benefit of the doubt. Why assume that teens are not just as capable of being honest and self-governing as adults? We laud children for their innocence—what is it about a teenager that makes them suddenly suspect?

Some would argue that it's simply memory. We recall all the hijinks we got into at "that age" and assume that kids must be just as wicked, if not more so. It's a kind of inverse nostalgia, and like the regular variety, it's a tender trap.

The initial temptation when designing a space for young adults to access the Internet is to make it as highly visible a space as possible. Place them at a clear plastic desk with a see-through monitor right in front of the reference desk. That's preventative maintenance really.

This is, of course, absurd, but that absurdity opens a door on the truth. Figuring out how to balance providing much needed educational and reference services offered by Internet terminals with leaving young adult patrons to use the Internet as their interests see fit is a challenge that every library must go through. The placement of Internet terminals can go a long way in striking that balance.

The first step is to take stock of the uses of the Internet terminals. Is there a "rush hour"? Do certain programs or services have high turnover? Do some young adult patrons simply camp out from the end of the school day until they're due home, or even until the library closes? Let's consider some of the concerns that face a department and how good design can help deal with them.

BEATING THE RUSH

The rush hour usually coincides with the end of the school day for the bulk of the year. During the summer or vacations, the rush can come at any time of day. From early in the morning, before summer jobs start or parents leave for the workday, to late afternoon when local parks and pools close down, the summer rush varies wildly.

In every case, the rush is simply a mass of young adult descending on the computers. Often this involves a lot of jumping around, clamoring, claiming of space, and general horseplay that comes with any excited group of teenagers rushing to claim a prize.

The rush can be dealt with in a few simple ways. First up, check-ins. As many library systems require some kind of electronic check-in (a card swipe, log-in, or other method), having a dedicated check-in spot for the computers is a sound idea. If possible, designate this check-in area with signage, and hang up the computer rules there as well. Make it clear how many patrons can share a computer and reinforce the idea that the person checking in is responsible for the computer and their area. Treating the space as if it were another item on loan from the library reinforces good policy as well as encourages individual responsibility. Emphasizing that you trust the teenagers is a step in the right directions.

RUINED BY RUNES

Like spam and the career of Cher, RuneScape will likely bury us all. The long lasting freeware MMO (massively multiplayer online game) has been running since 2001. Like the pay-for-play games of Warcraft™ and

Lord of the Rings online™, RuneScape is set in a fantasy world of myth and magic. Unlike those other intellectual properties, RuneScape is free to play, though there are paid accounts.

The game itself takes on the usual questing, collecting of items, and bartering. The appeal of the game lies largely in being free as well as accessible via login from anywhere in the world. A young adult can play at home, school, even the library, all without installing software.

RuneScape is not, in and of itself, disruptive. It's a game like any other. If anything the amount of focus and dedication shown by its players makes them less likely to be disruptive. They are, however, dedicated. Very dedicated.

I've personally seen young adults plop down at 3:15 P.M. and barely move from a computer, save for a bathroom break, until closing time. If they aren't roused or disturbed, they'll just keep playing.

This creates two problems for the library. First is the matter of a library computer devoted to gaming for hours at a time, something that can become an issue during the school year. The second is the matter of allowing a young person to engage in nearly addictive behavior without interruption.

Again, the question is how differently are we treating young adult patrons as compared to adults? Would we encourage an adult, perhaps hunched over an intense game of Scrabble™ or a research project, to get some fresh air and run around outside?

Avoiding this sticky question can be accomplished through some practical applications of design. First, consider designating specific computers for gaming. Place time limits, both on and off, those terminals for patrons. Say for every hour on, you can't register for two hours.

Also, consider not placing gaming computers away from other terminals. While it might seem counterintuitive, as games seem likely to cause distraction, the element of social interaction and lessening the screen-burn of isolating game play might work wonders.

RuneScape is just one of many freeware games. Facebook and other social media sites have opened up whole new realms of constantly evolving online play. For most young adults these games are a playful distraction, something to kill boredom or blow off steam.

Understanding that their use of these games isn't cause for fear about their intellection or ocular degradation is important, as many times the voices raised against gaming begin to sound shrill and hyperbolic. Just as most adults are able to be fully functional and keep up a mean minesweeper score, so too are young adults able to balance school and play.

HOW DO YOU SOLVE A PROBLEM LIKE MITCHELL?

In one of my first library positions there was a young patron whom I'll call "Mitchell," not his real name. Mitchell was 14, very bright, very friendly. He showed up at 3 P.M., exactly 10 minutes after the high school let out for the day, and he always signed up for one of the Internet computers. The computers were first come, first serve, and if there was someone waiting, there was a one-hour time limit. If there was no one waiting, it was an open buffet. Mitchell would play RuneScape, then go to any number of other flash-based game sites. He was a bright young kid who loved to brag about his latest online conquest or exploits.

Many nights it wasn't unusual for him to stay on the computer until we shut them down at nearly 9 P.M. Nearly six hours online, at least two or three days a week.

Mitchell caused a ruckus amongst the librarians for this behavior. There was concern for everything from his eyesight to his home life. Many staff members felt the library was "enabling an addiction" by allowing him to play for so long.

When a plan was hatched to limit the hours any young person could spend on a computer in a given day, the enforcement fell to me. Something felt deeply wrong about denying a patron access to a library service because it "wasn't good for him." There were times Mitchell would sit, arms folded, clearly bored, not far from the empty computers knowing that his time for the day was up.

So how do you address a problem like this? When you have open access, are you bound to allow some patrons to do themselves harm? For all the hysteria, was a young person playing online games any worse than watching television or movie? Could it be argued that at least games are interactive? Is the "arcade" aspect of games at the library a kind of embarrassment?

Some libraries try to address these issues by adopting strict usage policies, above and beyond any kind of filtering. Often these polices, sometimes backed up by site blocking, prohibit game sites altogether. The argument is that libraries serve a higher educational goal for young adults. Counterpoint to this is the argument that by limiting access and creating burdensome rules for using library computers, there is a chilling effect on overall library usage by young adults.

This is an issue with excellent arguments on both sides, but for our purposes let's look at the space planning solutions for this issues.

We've already talked about creating devoted spaces for gaming. What about the computers devoted to homework and research? Obviously preserving as much open access to these computers is paramount. In addition, reserving the right for patrons to enjoy a peaceful atmosphere is important as well. So creating policies in harmony with the design of the space is key.

One thing to keep in mind is the collaborative nature of many young adults' school projects. Whether it's a large-scale presentation or preparing with a partner for a standardized test, it's more than likely that young adults will be working in groups.

Computers are, by their very nature, designed to be used by a single user but consider setting up group-use computer stations if possible. Perhaps instead of using a carrel or computer desk, a large table could be set up with a computer? This prevents clumping around a single computer amongst the other single users.

Policies and access questions are never easy. While there are many good suggestions, finding out what works best for your patrons and your community is a matter of trial and error. The key is to strike a balance between the open access that libraries and librarians stand for, while keeping in mind the need to provide a safe and welcoming space for patrons with a wide variety of needs.

TO LISTEN AND SEE

Increasingly, entertainment is becoming a private affair. Multimedia devices offer users the ability to stream movies and music right in their hands, while major media companies struggle to further "monetize" large-scale entertainment.

Libraries have a unique position when it comes to multimedia technology. With the overlap of interlibrary loan, patrons the world over are limited only by the existence of a piece of media in what they can acquire and enjoy.

In creating spaces for young adults, an effort can be made to develop communal environments in which teens can enjoy multimedia programming within the library. It might sound old-fashioned, but a "listening station" might be a great addition to a young adult department.

In the early days of rock and roll, young people would cram into listening booths at record stores to hear the latest and greatest records. Recreating that exciting experience with modern technology is much easier, and there's no need to worry about scratching the records.

Consider creating a small set-off space with over-the-ear headphones hooked up to a digital collection of music. Keying in the collection to cataloging software could allow young adults to order or find music as they enjoy it. Hosting listening parties and music events, and spotlighting local artists in the listening room are all possibilities.

Televisions might, at first glance, seem anathema to the lofty literary goals of the library, but the notion that great works of art need to come from just the printed page is a very 20th-century prejudice.

Many librarians host movie nights and film events for patrons of all ages, but what about a dedicated movie space in the library?

With advances in camera and editing technology, more and more young adults are making their own films. Setting up a television that features local teen and young adult filmmakers along with Hollywood classics to inspire a new generation of creators is just one way to make great use of a television.

Consider that as HD and even 3-D televisions take hold, there will be a glut of older televisions coming into second-hand stores. A savvy young adult librarian could find large-screen television from the pre-digital era to suit any number of multimedia purposes.

OPERATOR? OPERATOR?

As was addressed earlier, cell phones have become a matter of fact for young adults. How can libraries tap into mobile devices to add to library spaces?

One, perhaps questionable, possibility is to look into "locations sensitive" technologies. A number of services are currently available that allow users to broadcast their location automatically. This, of course, has raised tremendous concerns about privacy. It puts one in mind of the dicey issue of whether to page a child to the phone for fear of becoming involved in problems at home. Broadcasting children's information across the net is seen, even by cooler heads, as a real worry.

Text messaging and picture/video messaging are also almost ubiquitous on mobile phone devices. More and more, teenagers are able to create, publish, and promote works of digital art and expression with a single device that fits in the palm of their hand. How can library spaces encompass this? By creating a "digital shadow" for the physical space.

Creating an online space for libraries is no longer simply about creating a Web site with links and hours. It's about tapping into the constant stream of information, expression, art, music, images, and videos created by young adults, and making them a part of the library.

As an example, say you wanted to promote science fiction books and movies over the course of a given month. You could encourage young adults to send digital images of science they see in the world around them to the library. Or ask students to contribute to an exquisite corpse–style story (where each person creates a new line of the tale) using text messages or tweets sent to the library. Help students create scavenger hunts that rely on photos and videos, or make stories based on random images featured in the library patron's photo stream. When designing or updating a space, whether on a temporary or permanent basis, call on young adults to send in picture ideas, video, and message as suggestions.

There are a great many simple checks and balances to keep material that is inappropriate from raising a ruckus from being seen.

Give teenagers a chance to play with their technological toys and use them to collaborate on enhancing library events and spaces. Creating a living digital shadow for the library space helps young adults, who are "born digital" feel more welcome.

ELECTROMAGNETIC DREAMS

Despite all this talk of technology, I suppose I am, deep down, a Luddite.

I have a deep and abiding romantic attachment to the loamy scent of the stacks. I love my eBook reader and iPod™, but you'll pry my hardcover from my cold dead fingers. For all the contributions of technology to libraries, I have the same worries that many do that in embracing the machine we lose a bit of ourselves in the process. It's a peevish and petty concern but it serves me well.

For all the techno-wizardry, touch-screens, and the like, the library is a space and a place. It's a destination. It is a destination that does well to evolve and grow with technology, but it's not just another place for screens and noise to fill up.

One of the most nefarious, and wonderful, devices I own is called a TV-B-Gone™. It's a simple black keyfob that has a single button. When pressed, this button cycles thorough hundreds of electronic signals to find just the right one to turn any TV in range off.

So many public spaces are filled with yammering, blaring televisions, most of which are shouting at no one in particular. As a bit of a nonscientific experiment I've turned off TVs in bars and restaurants, when no one was watching them of course, and seen just how little people actually miss the background noise.

There's a lesson in my little endeavor. Media is best when we are using it to the fullest. When it serves to simply fill the void with noise, it loses meaning, and perhaps we do as well.

If your patrons are making good and fruitful use of their Internet access, their multimedia devices, or if they are even tapping into the library's digital shadow, then technology can only enhance their enjoyment of the library.

It's when those technologies go underutilized or fail to connect with the everchanging needs of the patron base that it might be time to let the old cathode ray tubes cool down for a bit. Or whatever they put in those new-fangled iPhone thingees.

7
◇ ◇ ◇

MAKING ROOM ON A BUDGET

MONEY MATTERS AND OTHER TRUTHS

When it comes to matters monetary, I tend to come from the Dangerfield school of economic theory, the Rodney "I can't get no respect" Dangerfield school, to be precise.

The famed comic starred in a 1980s college romp called *Back to School*. Notable for its strange take on college life (including the excitable Sam Kinison as a professor), the film featured a memorable exchange between Mr. Dangerfield and a rather snooty economics professor.

The professor posited the creation of a fictional corporation and began to discuss taxes, permits, and zoning. Dangerfield countered with "real world" problems like bribes to officials, contractor disputes, and crooked politicians. The professor waved off these notions as the workings of a corrupt mind and then asked the class where they should build their factory. "How about Candyland?" came Dangerfield's retort.

It may seem flippant to compare the sober (and sobering) task of budgeting for libraries to an obscure 1980s comedy, but the points raised in that little exchange illustrate one of the greatest problems in any kind of budgeting: the disparities between what is planned, what is possible, and what actually happens.

Space is at a premium; furniture is expensive; library budgets are often whittled with a sharp and unforgiving blade by municipalities looking to trim "the fat." You need to be ready to defend your design, to make it cost effective and deal with the pitfalls, and pratfalls, that come with budgeting. This chapter will focus on developing a 10-point plan for evaluating, creating, budgeting, and defending a developed library space for teens and young adults. One you won't have to build in Candyland after all.

STEP ONE: A RUTHLESS SURVEY

Understanding exactly what your library already offers in terms of spaces for teens as well as what your collection can support (and be supported by) is the first step. Calling this a "ruthless" survey is more than just a swipe at wit. Much like the dreaded process of weeding, taking stock of where your library both succeeds and fails can be a galling process, though a revelatory one.

Begin with an assessment of the space you have. Does your library bifurcate between young adult and children's section already? At what age does this cut-off occur? Does the cut-off age work? This last question may be a very thorny one for many libraries. Some librarians may want a lower young adult cut-off age because they wish to focus on more younger oriented programming (lap sits, story times) while others may want a higher age to allow for family groups, siblings and the like, to stay together for longer. Again, it's a question that individual libraries must answer for their own patron base.

Surveying the space allotted is the next step. This may range from a simple pulling out of the measuring tape to a more involved process. One of the greatest wonders of the modern age of library planning is the simple digital camera. By taking detailed measurements along with photos from as many angles as possible, you can sit down and plan a space to a meticulous degree that would have been unthinkable even a generation prior.

STEP TWO: DOING MORE WITH LESS

Anyone familiar with the great HBO series *The Wire* has heard the phrase: "Do more, with less." It's a callous, almost mocking phrase that rings from the inner sanctums of politicians to the empty halls of public servants.

To many it might sound like a mantra for cutting corners. Serving off-brand soda at the staff luncheon, Zarex instead of Kool-Aid for the kids, not having as many programs in the week to cut back on hours. A great many libraries have cut full-time positions in twain to save on benefits or cut overall hours open to save on energy and staffing costs.

Doing more, with less. It's heart-wrenching for librarians for more than just our love of the profession, but because we know that libraries offer a unique public space, a third space between work and home, for all citizens. Those still locked out of the online era can get computer training at the library, or simply access job search sites and print resumes. Kids find refuge in libraries when things are hard at home. When parents are forced to prune expenses like music lessons, play groups or other after-school activities, the library is a welcoming alternative. Libraries have been doing more with less for a very long time.

When it comes to matters of design, how can we still get what we need while working with what we've got? Simple, pad the budget.

Now before you toss this book aside and demand my head for advocating fraud, let's take a moment to consider the sound financial wisdom of overage. When planning any kind of expansion, there are bound to be costs incurred by incidental actions. A contractor falling ill, an injury, turnover in a department, any number of a thousand little things can drive up the cost of a project. Budgeting a project tightly could end up damaging the project as a whole.

The better way is to be generous in your budget, within reason. It's not being dishonest; being prepared for the unexpected within any project is just sound financial planning. Adding a couple of hundred dollars to a furniture budget could make the difference between seating for 6 and a table for 10. You can do more with less, but don't sell the value of the library short in the hopes of low-balling a project's future.

STEP THREE: KNOW YOUR STAFF

I've spoken frequently about the value of any and all library staff. How a shelver can teach a degreed librarian more about the stacks with a few book trucks than some professors can rattle off in a whole course. Your staff is a gold mine of solid ideas about how to improve your library. At times there are interpersonal, political, and just downright petty differences that keep people from sharing their ideas. Someone who works the front desk might have a great idea for a display but they don't want to overstep their bounds. A librarian might have some notions to bring up before the board, but protocol calls for her to go through the chain of command. When designing a new space, these structures are only going to get in the way of the flow of good ideas.

Have a big open meeting for any and all staff. This might ruffle feathers of certain birds, but it's a place for everyone to present their ideas and have their voices heard in the plain clear light of day. This can cut down significantly on post-project grousing. Present the project as one that invites comment. Do the technical staff see any challenges to the new organization of young adult materials? Do the shelvers have ideas about how to encourage good patron return? Maybe the custodial staff has notions of how to save money on rewiring costs by making use existing electrical wiring. Serve food and drink and encourage free comment.

As the project takes shape, not every suggestion is going to be used, obviously. But keep staff informed on how the project is evolving, and perhaps explain why a given suggestion might not have worked or might be better for another situation. Keeping an open and free-flowing line of communication about any reorganization of a young adult space is going to make that space that much more popular with the staff, as well as with the patrons.

When the work is actually underway, you're going to need to tap into staff members for their expertise and support. This can cause some friction, like when the adult services staff are asked to cover the children's services desk during a contractor's visit, or desk staff find themselves dealing with patron complaints about the restructuring. Again, here's where open lines of communication become vital. When staff members have specific information, like when the construction will be ending or when material in transit might be back in circulation, they can provide patrons with better answers. Staff asked to work outside their usual area should be encouraged to try bringing some of their expertise to their assignment. Perhaps designing a display for the department or creating a bibliography, something where they can contribute their knowledge and they don't feel as if they are just being used as a human placeholder.

STEP FOUR: THE BODY POLITIC

Bringing your project up for review by a library board or other ruling body can be a nerve-wracking experience for any librarian. Perhaps you're lucky enough to have a board that is fully supportive of your endeavors, or maybe you're stuck with a board that questions every nickel and dime of even the most trivial expenditure. The old Boy Scout motto of "Be Prepared" never rings so true as when presenting your project, regardless of the audience.

First, consider what areas of the project might be problematic. Is there the possibility of a cost overrun? Has there been vandalism in the young adult area in the past so that the board worries about investing too much for fear of further damage? Is there a particular worry about noise or behavior issues with young adult patrons? Making sure you've thought about any issues before you face the board will make you all the more prepared.

Issues of money are often the most pressing to board members. It's often the case that library boards hold their duty as a public trust, and that they are responsible for making sure expenditures are reasonable and fair. Use that mindset to your advantage when pitching your project. Make it clear that a more attractive and well-designed space for young adults will not only increase use by that patron group, but also younger siblings and caregivers, all while continuing to foster a lifelong appreciation among teens for the library.

Along the same lines, it's always good to go in with concrete numbers. Explain how a well-developed teen space can increase circulation as well as programming attendance. Get numbers on how many young adults reside in your community as well as key circulation data relating to the target age range. Making correlations between the existing patron base and the possible base that could be served by an expanded teen space is a great way to get your point across.

Make your presentation as lively and tactile as possible. Much has been said over recent years about the dullness of PowerPoint presentations. Instead of projecting your numbers on a screen, make simple and clear handouts. Use pictures, videos, even simple models, to create a sense of how the space will be laid out. If you can, take the board to the area you're looking to develop, walk them through the changes and how you see the space evolving to feed the needs of the young adult population.

Finally, make sure you understand the timing of your board. Sometimes new business is tabled until certain grants or monies are available and sometimes it's simply a matter of internal politics as to when a new project will be considered. Following up and understanding their timetable is simply part of the process. Don't be alarmed if the wheels grind slowly; just be sure to keep an eye out that they haven't ground to a halt.

STEP FIVE: LAUNCH (OR FAILURE TO)

Your project is a go! Funding has been allocated, staffing has been rearranged, the calendar is clear, and the new teen space is ready to start. Then why does it seem that everything is going wrong?

Perhaps it's the contractor who gives a quote then backtracks forcing you to recalculate your entire budget. Maybe it's the IT department pointing out that the computer terminals are going to be too far from the wall jacks. It could be that the company who makes the perfect booth seating for your teen alcove has just doubled their price, or gone out of business, or wants to charge so much for shipping you might as well go and pick it up yourself.

It's the start of a brave new adventure, so why is everything going wrong?

Any complex endeavor is bound to run into a number of problems along the way. When you're dealing with not just the politics of the library, but financing, vendors, contractors, staffers, and any number of other individuals, you're bound to hit a snag. Or a number of snags.

The key here is to take each setback in stride and be ready with a backup plan. Remember your overall goal is to develop a highly interactive space for young adults that is adaptive and reactive. If you don't get just the right study carrel or the exact kind of laminate for your booth or your favorite shade for the massive beanbag chairs, take the matter in stride.

Librarians tend toward fastidiousness; it's the very nature of the profession really. Telling a librarian not to get hung up on the details is a bit like telling a surgeon not to worry about all the organs. But remember that keeping the big picture goal in mind can help keep your sanity, even when it seems that is a rare commodity amongst those you are dealing with.

So keep your head and keep your momentum in the forward direction. A good way to keep that momentum is to set smaller goals along the way. If your restructuring involves a large amount of construction or rebuilding, make a progress marker somewhere in the center of the library where patrons and staff can keep up to date.

Another way to keep things positive is to fully document the progress of the project with photos and videos. These not only keep those involved in the work motivated, but they provide the curious (and perhaps the doubtful) with substantive evidence of the progress being made. It's one thing to doubt a proposal; it's another to scoff at a work in progress.

Motivation not only helps the current project, but also excites the community about the library's growth and overall health. Discovering that the library is redeveloping a space for young adults may help sell development for more elder care services or programs for recent immigrants or young families. Tapping into your community's curiosity as a means of motivation is a great benefit to everyone.

STEP SIX: OVERAGES AND UNDER

Even the most careful plan is likely to run into budgetary issues. Whether it is a change in local government that leads to a cut in funding, a singular board member driving for a shift in priorities or a an overall economic downturn, no project is wholly safe from the vicissitudes of fate and the long knives of the accountants.

Any sound plan should include an overage of at least 10 percent, a simple bit a math even easier to calculate than a tip at a restaurant. A $2,000 project should be quoted as a $2,200 project. On the surface, this seems like a bad idea to many nervous types. The old fear that "If we ask for too much we'll never get what we need." This approach is foolhardy.

Let's take a hypothetical approach. Say that a reorganization of the young adult books and shelving area works out to around $1,500. The cost is quoted to the director and board and the money allocated for new shelving, displays, and other expenses; however, it turns out that the shelves ordered are of a low-quality particle board material that, while attractive enough in samples and catalogs, looks cheap and feels flimsy once in place. A replacement can be found but is slightly more expensive.

If no overage is planned, the department must now go to the board, hat in hand, and explain the situation, which in turn could lead to questions about the ordering process, the planning, the provider and a whole host of other complications that do little to serve the end goal. In short, it creates a hassle for all involved.

With an overage, the department can avoid the mess and bring the project in at budget. Now, what if the project comes in under budget? This is something that I think any librarian worth their weight in books would call a "high-class problem." Which is to say, how often do you really hear someone complaining about having too much money?

Say that in the previous hypothetical that the shelves had come in not only in fine condition but also at a discount rate compared to what was originally planned. Perhaps a more expensive model has superseded your selection and yet your original choice still offers all the original features at a reduced price. This brings the project in under budget, which in your final report to the board can serve only to bespeak the excellent planning that went into your project. It's never a bad thing to save a public organization a little bit of money.

Careful budgeting has the ancillary benefit of allowing the department to weather shifts in the political and economic climate as well. A new mayor may cut library funding, or perhaps an old board member who took up the cause of the library has chosen to retire after decades of service. Being able to deal with, as the Bard said, the slings and arrows of outrageous fortune, is something that only serves to benefit any project overall.

On a purely reputation-based note, it's always a fine thing for librarians to be looked at as being overprepared rather than caught flat-footed. It's something of a compliment to our meticulous nature.

STEP SEVEN: OH THE MESSES YOU'LL MAKE

When I was in my senior year of high school, I oversaw the construction of sets for a production of *You're a Good Man Charlie Brown*. My vision, such as it was, was simple—to use large panels of plaster as the backdrop. This gave the whole stage the look of a comic book panel, honoring the roots of the *Peanuts*-inspired musical. The plasterboard pieces were huge and cutting them into shape, sanding, and painting them took weeks and made a royal mess. At one point the principal of the school, a nun with a rather fearsome way about her, toured our stage. She looked as if she was sniffing something that smelled particularly rotten and, just before she left, looked at me and said, "Young man, I hope this play is worth all the clean-up you'll be doing." Any sort of change, whether it's as simple as moving some furniture or a complex rewiring of the entire library computer system, is going to cause some degree of mess. Even if the fracas only last a few days, there's bound to be some confusion, misdirection, and inevitably complaints about the goings-on.

There exists a mythological construct of the library as a place of eternal solemnitude. In some respects, this is true. Libraries can be quiet refuges of peaceable learning, a truism many librarians cultivate. Libraries are also busy, bustling places, an ideal many more librarians strive for. But when a library becomes a place where the quietude is breached and the bustling gives way to the sounds of construction, there's bound to be a certain bit of rancor rising from patrons.

The best way to ameliorate the more contentious patron's surly response is to give them ample warning. Making patrons aware well ahead of time that disruption in service is coming and letting them know the times it's happening so they can best avoid it is vital. Postings on the library Web site in addition to signage throughout the library well ahead of any project will help stem the tide.

Of course there will always be those who view any change or interruption as an affront; they may question the cost or the timing (regardless of when you go about it), whether in person or through some other means. Again, communication is the key. Preparing staff to answer questions with solid information about the project, when any service interruptions will occur, and what the ultimate benefits will be for the library and community can offset any grumbling.

Scheduling large-scale projects carefully, keeping in mind things like peak usage time and school breaks and vacations can avoid a great deal of consternation. Using school libraries and home-schooler networks to spread the word about any changes in service can help prepare patrons as well.

Regardless of the mess you have on your hands at the moment, keeping the public aware of any changes that might impact their library service is simply good librarianship. Even the most questioning patron can be made understand that while at the moment there's a bit of racket in the young adult section, in a month's time their teenage daughter will have a whole new multimedia center or study center.

STEP EIGHT: ALERT THE MEDIA

The saddest party in the world is one nobody knows about. Treat the gestation and delivery of your teen space like it's the biggest party since the millennium. Bigger even, since you won't have all those math geeks arguing that it really wasn't the millennium until 2001.

Never underestimate the power of a snappy press release. Writing up your project in glowing terms, with quotes from board members, librarians, and even patrons, and sending it off to local print media outlets is one cheap and simple way to get coverage. Reaching beyond print, be sure to share photographs and video on the library Web site. Use social networking sites to spread the word far and wide.

The suffusion of video in the culture is such that it seems almost comic. It seems that every new gadget is also a high-end digital camera of some kind. This has been combined with the dawn of streaming video online, allowing anyone with even the most basic of tech to become a broadcaster. The net effect of this is an expectation from interested people, and from young people in particular, for digital video to be part of any presentation. In short, if you're advertising to young adults, you better be advertising with video.

Creating a short commercial video might seem daunting to those not of the "digital native" generation. Perhaps there's a fear of looking cheesy or silly. Keep in mind that a promotional video the library creates is essentially a news story over which the library has full editorial control. That alone should be a selling point for those nervous about becoming the next comic meme.

Keeping it simple is the key in any advertising. A press release should be short, snappy, and to the point. The Appendix provides a sample press release that you can adapt to suit your needs. With a video, keeping it short (2–3 minutes at the most) and focused is vital. Show details, not talking heads. Make use of limited voiceover and make use of public domain music to avoid issues with posting on video sites like YouTube™ or Vimeo™.

It may sound a bit like cheating, but another way to advertise without breaking the bank is to create a contest for young adults to create their own commercial or advertisement. Offer the use of library facilities and technology, and make the contest into a program teaching about communication and promotions.

Outreach to schools is another method of advertising that is critical to the success of any project. Reaching out to school librarians and teachers to incorporate the new teen space into their lesson plans and activities is a way to boost use and get fresh faces into the library. You might have drawn them in via schoolwork, but hopefully your space will keep them coming back.

STEP NINE: TAKE CREDIT AND ASSESS BLAME

All right, you're not really going to blame anyone, but an honest self-evaluation is critical to the process of any large project. It's not healthy to dwell on the "could-have-been" or "never-was" aspects of a project. Yes, it would have been nice if the library board had approved a $10,000 expenditure instead of just $7,500. Of course, it would have been lovely if the bond issue had passed and the new library did not need a mortgage. And yes, the booths were not the exact color that the committee wanted. Things operating "above your pay grade" as it were are often at play while you are hard at work.

Honest assessment comes from looking at what has been accomplished versus what the original intent was at the outset. If your initial intent was to create a "welcoming space for young adults to access technology and socialize," does your space provide that? Perhaps that intent is not specific enough. Perhaps you wanted a space that could comfortably accommodate up to 15 young adults at time, and you find that, with all the alterations along the way, it's really best for just 10 teens at any given time. Can anything be done to deal with this, or is it simply to way things have to be?

One thing to avoid at this point is finger pointing. If things have come up short, whether a minor quibble over design or a major conflict regarding the project's outcome, it's important to focus on the practical and not get bogged down in blame.

Review the process as it unfolded. Look at how the initial proposal could have been better presented. How could the staff have been better prepared or contributed to the design and concept process? Was there a lack of input from a given group within the library? Were there outside pressures that could have been mitigated, or, alternately, listened to as sound advice? What steps could have been taken during the building process? What can be done to address nagging concerns?

All these questions, and as many more as your unique project and community require, should be looked at as honest inquiry and straightforward assessment. It's not about shaming anyone; it's about finding where the process worked and where it did not so that the future can only be bigger, better, and brighter.

Though this is not to say that all self-assessment is a form of self-flagellation. There's no reason not to believe your designs and plans won't exceed expectations in any number of ways. Here to, it is vital to be honest in your assessment. There's an old saw that while many athletes will watch game films after a loss, it's the champions who watch after a win. Understanding your success can only help you repeat it.

Perhaps the most clearheaded way to approach assessment is to look at it from a scientific mindset. If an experiment failed, it's worth documenting carefully so as not to repeat the same mistakes. If it succeeded, you want to be able to share your success and repeat it under new circumstances.

Success is said to have a thousand fathers but failure is an orphan. When it comes to assessing your project, think of the stereotypical 1950s nuclear family. Strive for a happy home with the occasional tense dinner conversation but never a raised voice.

STEP TEN: BEST PRACTICES FOR ALL

If there's one thing librarians excel at, it's sharing information. When it comes to best practices, we librarians become one big happy gossiping clan. Sharing your experience with other librarians is a way of not only tooting your own horn, but also helping the library community as a whole. Your experiences could prove invaluable to librarians who are in similar situations.

Pick your electronic poison. Whether it's submitting a write-up to an e-mail list, posting a "behind the scenes" podcast interview, or reaching out to any number of library publications, there's no small number of ways to share your experience.

Conferences, large and small, are excellent places to talk about your endeavors. Don't be intimidated by the slick stylings of many presenters. Some of the most earnest and interesting presentations I've come across at conferences came from librarians with decidedly low-fi approaches to presentation.

An anecdote I often share concerns the first librarian conference I attended after leaving grad school. It was a conference of school librarians with dozens of panels and hundreds of exhibitors. I freely confess to being overwhelmed by the sheer hugeness of the experience and more than a little lost. Carrying the requisite "bag of swag," I wandered like a tourist, drinking it all in.

Towards the end of the first day, I found a small conference room to duck into and rest my feet. A presentation was just starting up given by a pair of librarians from Kentucky. They didn't have any video or handouts. Their presentation consisted of pictures and prepared remarks. And yet, I was bowled over. These librarians had taken a small grant of just $2,500 and used it to completely remodel their young adult reading area. They talked about building relationships with business in their small town and how those relationships helped them negotiate deals for everything from furniture to food for their volunteers shifting books over one long weekend.

What made their presentation work was the sincerity of it. They had taken an idea, made it work for them, fitting the unique needs and character of their community and library. They were honest in their assessment and ultimately ended up with a project that exceeded expectations.

Perhaps you've heard of the 1960s rock band the Velvet Underground? Their experimental style grew out of Andy Warhol's art Factory in New York. The band was never much of a commercial success, but their work served to inspire many up and coming artists. The legendary musician Brian Eno once remarked while very few people bought the band's records, all who did ended up forming bands of their own.

So whether you choose to share your success or not is your call, but keep in mind that one good idea, shared with the right people, could help form a thousand more. Just remember, you could be the Velvet Underground of young adult librarianship. That would impress even the most jaded teenager.

8

◆◇◆

A TALE OF TWO SPACES

It's true, we really can have too much of a good thing. One of the more confounding aspects of preparing for a major overhaul of a library space can be the surplus of information. Only a few years ago, librarians "only" had numerous journals, magazines, and the beginnings of online communities to rely on. Now you can spends months sifting through podcasts, blogs, multimedia presentations from conferences, and any number of social networks. There's so much good information about best practices that it's almost an impediment to putting those practices in to practice.

One good metric is to look for a library of approximately the same size that has developed their young adult space. While your community might have very different needs, at very least you have a rough sense of scale.

This chapter will cover two young adult spaces built in recent years. One serves one of the largest American cities, and the other serves a city in New Zealand of just over 120,000 residents. Both spaces have been developed according to the unique needs of their respective communities and serve as great benchmarks for designing effective young adult spaces.

DUNEDIN CITY LIBRARY TEEN SPACE

Dunedin, New Zealand, is a city rich with natural beauty and architectural splendor. Settled by Europeans in the mid-19th century, the area had been long occupied by Maori with settlements stretching back some 700 years. Careful readers of that study-hall bible the *Guinness Book of World Records* may recognize Dunedin as the home of the world's steepest street. It's Baldwin St., for those looking to stretch their legs. The city is famed for its many architectural treasures including First Church and the campus of University of Otago.

Dunedin's public library is made up of five branches spread through out the city. The City Library branch is the first public library that opened in the city, in 1908. Interestingly, the library was founded with funds from famed American library benefactor Andrew Carnegie. It is in this historic branch that we find the exemplary Teen Space, which opened in 2008, a century after the library's founding.

Beginning in 2002, the library began outreach to understand what the young adults of their community wanted from a teen library space. Some of the suggestions included

- Couches, beanbags, cushions
- Listening posts with a choice of music
- Somewhere to crash
- TV with DVDs
- Somewhere to study
- Staff, but not in the space itself
- Somewhere to eat

The library staff also consulted local youth councils, made up of young adults aged 14 to 24. The comments gathered and input from young adult patrons directly impacted the design of the teen spaces from the very start.

The space itself is fairly large (measuring 52' x 35') and is twice the size of the former teen space. In preparing the space for the young adults, the decision was made to give the space as different a look from the rest of the library as possible. The drop ceiling was removed to reveal ductwork and overhead fixtures, something commonly seen in hip high-end loft apartments. The lighting fixtures themselves include designer lampshades and a chandelier from a second-hand supplier.

In furnishing the space, the library chose to take a decidedly "retro" approach, relying on second-hand stores and auction houses. This is not to say the furniture isn't stylish. With bright colors, including a bright orange couch, as well as retro 1970s kitchen chairs, the space takes on the look of a hip coffeehouse. Twelve large and colorful beanbag chairs are scattered through the space. A foosball table is also found in the space.

Technology suffuses, but does not overwhelm, the Teen Space. A wide-screen TV with wireless headphones receives a selection of TV channels, including Maori television. Four listening stations with streaming Internet audio options and cordless headphones allow teens to listen to a wide variety of music and audio programming. Computer terminals offering access to library services were also placed in the space.

The intent of the space is clear, to give the young adults of Dunedin a place that feels both social and yet personal. The comparison can easily be made to a teenager's bedroom, a sanctum that is also a place young adult often like to hang out in with friends. The placement of the reference desk, just outside the Teen Space but not in the actual space, conveys a sense of public/privacy. Security cameras monitor the space, something increasingly common in public libraries.

In publicizing the launch of their space in 2008, timed to coincide with New Zealand National Youth Week, the staff of the Dunedin library ran into the issue of how to publicize to teens. Finding their usual methods of advertising coming up short, the library staff learned how teens use their own unique social networks (both online and off) to communicate. For example, the teen musicians who are invited to perform at a space often bring their own audience.

Since its opening the Teen Space has become a regular venue for young adult musicians. It's also been host to dance troupes and author workshops. The space has been used for art exhibitions and even as a set for young adults shooting short films.

I chose to highlight Dunedin's excellent teen space not just for the size of the community, but because the Dunedin library carefully documented the construction of the Teen Space online with digital photos. Showing the development of the space, in this case using a gallery on the photo-hosting site Flickr, is extremely helpful to anyone looking to put the best practices of the Teen Space to use in their library. Archiving the process is a valuable tool not only for other libraries, but also as a means of self-diagnostic.

The real success of the Teen Space is in developing a multipurpose space that, while providing for and meeting the stated needs of the young adult patron base, is still open enough to evolve and grow.

Regardless of the size of your library project, the Dunedin multi-purpose provides some key best practices worth adopting.

- Tapping into young adults for their sense of how the space should be designed is critical to making the space a success.
- Creating an open space that can be easily re-purposed for any number of library events allows a space to evolve as the needs of the teen patrons change.
- A space that is unique, fun, and visually different from the rest of the library is one that will appeal to young adults and allow them to own the space as their own.

Meeting the needs of a diverse population is a challenge for any library, and young adults present a special challenge in their often-shifting interests and needs. In designing a space with the direct input of the young adult population, the Dunedin Teen Space didn't need to rely on guesswork about fads to understand their patrons needs.

CHICAGO PUBLIC LIBRARY YOUMEDIA CENTER

The Chicago Public Library (CPL) is one of the largest and most diverse library systems in the United States. With nearly 80 branches throughout the city, CPL serves the millions of Chicagoans yearly. The CPL has been in a period of rapid growth over the past 20 years, opening nearly 52 new libraries since 1989. The central library of the system is the Harold Washington Library, located in downtown Chicago. This massive structure, the size of a city block, is home to the YOUMedia center.

The YOUMedia center is a massive (5,500 square foot) space on the first floor of the library. YOUMedia opened in 2009 and was the culmination of a three-year project. The space was funded in large part by a $500,000 grant from the John D. and Catherine T. MacArthur Foundation. An additional $180,000 in technology funding came from the Pearson Foundation working with the Chicago Public Library Foundation. The space was designed by graduate students working with the Carnegie Mellon University Entertainment Technology Center. The project as a whole was a collaboration between the CPL and the Digital Youth Network, a digital literacy program that works with young people in and out of school settings.

It's clear from the start of the discussion that this project is one that has excited a whole host of nonprofit and charitable foundations. The space itself is truly worth al the "buzz" it generated.

YOUMedia is broken up into several distinct spaces, each offering young adults a different experience.

Hang Out: Described on the YOUMedia site as a "landing area." This space is focused on the social. A space where teens can hang out, eat snacks, use computers to check e-mail, or read. The hang out space is also the gathering point for workshops that provide introductions to the technological resources available at YOU-Media and other group projects.

Mess Around: Moving on from the landing area, this is a space set up for young adults to explore digital media. YOUMedia provides digital cameras (video and still) as well as gaming stations, audio recording equipment, and laptops for teens looking to explore and play. This area allows teens the freedom to work with the equipment without the structure of a class or program. It's also an area for young adults who have gone through workshops to continue their work.

Geek Out: The most structured aspect of the YOUMedia space is for those teens ready to participate in media training. Classes and workshops, led by librarians as well as YOUMedia mentors, give young adults a full range of training. There are introductory classes in handling digital equipment and advanced workshops for older and more experienced young adults to sharpen their skills and gain more hands-on experience.

In all, YOUMedia features over 100 computers. The space also includes a recording studio for musicians or budding digital broadcasters. A wide-screen television with the latest generation consoles can also be found in the space; located in the hang out area, it's a popular and attractive part of the "crash" space. Game design is one of the many educational workshops that YOUMedia offers. Workshops in game design affords those playing games now a chance to create something even better in the future.

The Chicago Public Library's connections with the Chicago Public School system obviously run deep, and the CPL has reached out to teachers to encourage them to bring classes to the YOUMedia center. This not only serves the educational goals of the school, but also acts as a form of community outreach and awareness raising among young adults.

YOUMedia also serves as a performance space, both for visiting musicians and the talented young adults creating their own new media on site. Book talks, reader's circles, and author visits are also held in the space.

Workshops offered at YOUMedia for high school students cover a wide range of digital and "analog" topics. Learning about digital video editing, creating podcasts and digital publishing, as well as writing fan fiction and general graphic design are all topics covered in workshops. The mentors and librarians on staff at YOUMedia work with teacher and young adults in the space to get them up and running on independent projects.

YOUMedia's cutting-edge technological toys might seem to over-shadow the, seemingly old-fashioned, books, but the space is filled with thousands of books and circulation has gone up since the opening. Highly interesting young adult fiction, including graphic novels and popular series, are highlighted throughout the space.

The digital shadow cast by YOUMedia is enormous. The space has it's own dedicated Web site, listing everything from upcoming events and a layout of the space to digital media created on site by young adults.

The YOUMedia space is the envy of libraries large and small. Partner-ship with endowing organizations and educational institutions allowed the CPL to defray costs and create a more vibrant and exciting space.

- A small community library might look at YOUMedia as the unat-tainable, but even on a limited budget there are best practices worth emulating.

- Creating separate and dedicated spaces for activities helps to keep a sense of order and allows young adults to choose how they wish to spend their time.

- Not tying the use of library facilities and tech too tightly to library programming is a way of allowing teenagers to explore digital media at their own pace. While your library might not have a 100 computers on hand, it's a rather simple matter to devote one or two (perhaps older) computers to simple online tasks like check-ing e-mail and social networks.

A WORLD APART?

Choosing one library in a thriving American megapolis to compare with another library in a mid-sized New Zealand city seems to be a rather transparent attempt to pick libraries as far afield as possible. These two libraries are, almost literally, on opposite sides of the planet.

And yet, their needs are very much the same. Both Dunedin and Chi-cago have young adults who are looking for a unique space where they can use and explore media on their own. Whether that media is as high tech as a tiny digital camera, or as simple as a great book, it's about finding a space that they are comfortable in.

Take note that in both libraries the young adults have a space where adults are present, but a bit distant. In Dunedin it's the reference desk placed just outside the Teenspace; in Chicago it's a hang out area for casual use. Teens can assert their independence and yet, in the same breath, ask that they not be left completely on their own after all. Again, the importance of respecting that delicate line between adult and young adult becomes clear.

Taking inspiration from either of these successful library spaces is a good start to any project. It is a phrase I've heard time and again amongst programming librarians: "Copying success is the highest compliment." Whether you end up with a massive multimedia center or a humbler raw space might be a matter of budgeting, but no matter your financial situation, you can maximize your return on investment by wisely "complimenting" successful library spaces.

FURTHER READING

About Us. *You Media.* 2010. http://youmediachicago.org/2-about-us/pages/2-about-us.

Ikin, Su. Our Library Their Space: the Dunedin City Library Teen Space.—Free Online Library. *Free Online Library.* June 1, 2010. http://www.thefreeli brary.com/Our library their space: the Dunedin City library Teen Space. a0231313206.

Project of the Week: YOUmedia (Chicago Public Library). *GovLoop—Social Network for Government.* April 16, 2010. http://www.govloop.com/profiles/blogs/project-of-the-week-youmedia.

"Teenspace Opening 08—A Set on Flickr." *Welcome to Flickr—Photo Sharing.* http://www.flickr.com/photos/dunedinpubliclibraries/sets/72157605238494567/.

9

◇ ◇ ◇

MAKING ROOM,
CHANGING LIVES

GETTING PERSONAL

Growing up, a library saved my life. Really, it did.

While this might immediately set off the hyperbole detector of a reasonable person, it is, in fact the truth.

I grew up on the far northwest side of the city of Chicago as an only child, whose widowed mother worked crazy hours just to keep a roof over our heads and shoes on our feet. Most of my childhood was spent in alleyways and city parks. Running down hot summer sidewalks, chasing ice cream trucks with a handful of pocket change, or trudging home from school in the sludge mess of a Chicago winter, that's what I like to remember.

What I don't like to remember was getting picked on by the bullies and tough kids in my neighborhood and at my school. The fights, often one-sided, and taunts are hard to forget, even years later. Many days I'd come home, to an empty house, bruised in body and soul, to sulk. My standing order was to call my mom and let her know I was home safe and sound. Putting on a brave face, or in this case voice, was something I learned to do quite young. I didn't want to add to her worries with my worries.

My Aunt Nora was a librarian at my grade school. Her home was filled with books, and it seemed only a matter of logic that she ended up a librarian. She was a stern, not quite embodying the stereotype of the "shush-ing" librarian, but she was certainly strong tea. On days when it was truly horrid outside, my cousins and I would catch a ride from my aunt after school. This meant sitting in the school library after hours while she wrapped up the day.

I say "school library," but in actuality the space was called the "Learning Center." It included a big open carpeted pit where we would watch movies and filmstrips. Sitting in the grey carpeted pit watching *Davey and Goliath* while waiting for my aunt to finish indexing the day's book checkouts and re-shelve the paperbacks was something of a winter staple.

So my impressions of a library weren't all that impressive. It was a place you waited for other things to happen. It was limbo, with your aunt pestering you to lend a hand and organize a book cart.

But when I was 11 years old, a library saved my life.

It was the summer of 1990, and I was being chased on foot by a pack of the meanest kids from my school. It was the last day of school and a time when all scores were to be settled. I was the somewhat mouthy chubby kid and apparently I was way over due for a savage beating. I remember running so hard and so fast that I seemed to be using my asthma inhaler the same way a street racer might use a nitrous boost. I tried ducking into the 7-Eleven, the comic store, even the McDonald's, all to no avail. These guys were going to wait me out and knock me out.

Finally, I reached the Albany Park branch of the Chicago Public Library at the intersection Foster and Kimball avenues. They might as well have hung a banner saying "Shangri-La" or "Valhalla" over the doors. Here I could hide out. No bully, no matter how crass or dangerous would start a fight in a library! Such an act was tantamount to sacrilege. An irony, since all involved parties, bullies and bullied, were altar servers at the local Catholic church.

More than two decades later, I can remember how relieved I was to hit that air conditioning, to be surrounded by books, to look back at the baleful faces of my pursuers and know that I was safe and sound. I had found refuge; I could throw my hands up and cry out "Sanctuary! Sanctuary!" in the finest imitation of Quasimodo and find it within the stacks.

Ah, yes, the hyperbole detector just buried the needle.

But that's not how the library saved my life.

There was a librarian who saw me come barreling through the doors, careen past the alarm gates, and stand, goggle-eyed, in the entryway. She walked over to me and asked if I was all right. I told her I was fine, and she, of course, did not believe me. The librarian, whose name I'm sorry to say is lost to my memory, spent about 10 minutes walking me around the library, before sitting me down in part of the adult section filled with *Doctor Who* paperbacks and some fellow nerds. None of them had a wolf pack of bullies on their heels, but we did commiserate on the experience.

I spent a lot of that summer in the library. I signed up for the summer reading program and came in second in a mystery-themed costume contest. I wandered the adult stacks and ended up carving out a mini young adult section with friends I met at the library, made up largely of those fellow traveler nerds. I played a role-playing game for the very first time, learned how to use a computer, and read my way through huge chunks of Stephen King's oeuvre.

That summer changed my life. The library gave me place of refuge and a place where I could geek out with friends for hours on end. I wasn't a kid in the alleyways anymore or bored in a carpeted pit. I was someone at my library. When I graduated high school and college and graduate school, each time my mother would, at some point amidst the festivities, mention how the library was what saved me. "You had a place to go, and I knew you were safe and having good fun."

"Good fun." That was her way of saying I wasn't getting into fights or sitting alone in the house or any of the other wonderfully dangerous possibilities that await a curious 11-year-old on the streets of Chicago.

I had some friends, from similar backgrounds, who didn't end up getting a graduate degree. Or a college degree. A couple of them never even made it out of high school. A good friend ended up in a gang and later, in jail. We came from the same neighborhood, but I found refuge in the library, and they found something else to fill their days. The results were very different.

WHY WE DO WHAT WE DO

"Well, OK, we get it. Libraries are great. Aren't you preaching to the choir on this? Is your story all that miraculous, all that special?"

No, it's not. Not at all. That's the point. For many young adults, any young adult, a library can be the place that makes the difference. A library can change the world of a young person at a time when their world is in almost constant flux. The library can be stable ground when it seems everything has turned to quicksand.

The library I spent my time in didn't have a dedicated teen space. The space was divided between "Children" and "Adult" by the very design of the structure. The building dated from the early 1960s, a time when the line between adult and child was seen more as a border and less as a territory.

This didn't stop the librarians from helping the young adults find a niche, or making a space for programming. Even when challenged by the space, they found a way to make us welcome, to keep us coming back. They did it because they knew what every librarian who works with young adults knows, that it's so easy to lose teens to the whirlwind of distractions.

It's why we do what we do. The plain truth of the world is that when you become a young adult, you're freer to be distracted. There's less structure to guide you to good choices. Choices like reading and engaging programming and making friends in an environment that encourages creativity and excitement.

You don't necessarily always have the steady hand to guide you. Parents and teens engage in the age-old battles, and to flout their independence, many young adults make bad decisions. As they get older, the consequences for these choices become more and more severe.

This is not to say that we do what we do out of fear, but rather out of hope. The right book in the hands of the right child can reshape the world. How many future lawyers did *To Kill a Mockingbird* inspire? How many astronauts started their adventures with Ray Bradbury or Harlan Ellison? In decades to come, how many artists and performers will look back on the works of J. K. Rowling as their first inspiration. We know the power books and stories have to shape lives; it runs to the very core of librarianship.

Creating a space where those introductions can take place is our challenge. It may seem the stuff of fancies to worry about beanbag and retro furniture, but what you're really doing is setting a stage.

YOUR STAGE IS THEIR KINGDOM

Pardon me for the metaphorical gamesmanship, but think of your teen space as stage, upon which a most important play will be performed. The scenery should enhance the story, but not distract from the action. The space should allow for movement, because the players are bringing their finest moves to the performance.

But this play is not for anyone's entertainment. Young adults are natural performers, they're in the midst of a great work of theater, their day-to-day lives. Teens craft their personas the same way great actors do. A great teen space gives them a place to try on their personas in a safe and welcoming environment.

The most common, and cranky, complaint about teens is that they are noisy, rambunctious, problem patrons. In the course of my career, my most common reply to this handwringing is to simply say, "Yeah, but they're *in the library*." While that may sound absolutely rife with the snark and sarcasm too often wielded by young adults themselves, it's a truism. What better setting is there for young people to explore and be boisterous and excited and joyful than the library? It's up to us to create a space that they can use, own, and ultimately respect.

MAKING ROOM

Making room for teenagers in your library is about so much more than just shifting the young adult paperbacks and tables. It's a change in mindset. Much of the preceding chapters have been about getting the mindset right as much as the masonry. It's about creating a space that is also an idea. That may sound like something more likely found on a fortune cookie, or coming out of the mouth of Morpheus from *The Matrix*, but it's true all the same.

Librarians as "information scientists" are dedicated to the systemization of knowledge as well as the free and open access to that knowledge for all. It's the bare bones of what being a librarian is all about. Providing access to teens is as much about what you offer on the shelves as the space those shelves are found in. What good are the greatest young adult works of the past decade if young adults have to find them in an austere adult section? How inviting is a book discussion for *Catcher in the Rye* when you're holding it in a room decorated to appeal to toddlers?

To use a buzz phrase that I dislike but find so very appealing, here's your "take away": *Making room for teens is not about separation, it's about access.*

It's not about creating fancy spaces or using hip technology, it's about providing young adults with a place where their voice can be heard. It's about providing them with a space where they can access information in an environment that welcomes them, that reaches out to them as patrons and provides for their unique service needs.

The sad fact is that as long as there are rowdy teenagers and scare stories about them, whether blown up in the media or just passed around as gossip, there will always be some opposition to granting teenagers a space of their own. Some people oppose spaces for young adults out of fear, others for vaguely defined moral reasons. I've sat, trying very hard not to laugh, as a patron excoriated me on the "lascivious nature" of beanbag chairs.

Another patron told me, without batting an eye, that kids from ages 12 to 18 shouldn't be allowed in the library because they're "up to no good."

Even years after the fact, these, and dozens of other encounters, still ring in my head. They're the outliers, sure, but they can be noisy outliers. Young adults are a lightning rod for controversy, and strong opinions are often proffered regardless of the facts.

That's why committing to the creation of viable spaces for young adults goes beyond simple good marketing and good design. Making room for teens is about making the library as a whole a more accessible and open place. It's about building a bridge from children's to adult programming and collection development. It's about sustaining and nurturing a generation of lifelong learners and readers.

The phrase "cradle to grave" is often thrown around in hot-button political discussions. Libraries serve just that "demographic." From those seated in their parent's lap to patrons steadied by their great-grandchildren, libraries serve all ages. Making room for teens, whose unique energy and perspicacity touches patrons of all age groups, is not just an investment in the success of libraries today, but a sound plan for building libraries as community centerpieces for decades to come.

A long time ago, a library saved my life. If you make room for young adults in your library, just imagine the lives you could touch, shape, and, perhaps, even save.

APPENDIX

Date: (Today's Date)

For Immediate Release   **Contact:** Joe Q. Bibliophile
Young Adult Librarian
(555) 555-5555
Example City Announces New Teen Space

Opening Ceremony and Concert, July 1

Example City—The Example City Library has a whole new place just for teens. Starting July 1, Teen Space, will open in the main branch of the Example City Library, offering young adults a fun and exciting new space.

Designed in conjunction with area high school students, the Teen Space has been built from the ground up as a great place for area young adults.

"We worked closely with students to create a fun and vibrant space," says Director Shawn Biblioteca "Teen Space is a place where young adults can congregate, create, and explore all the library has to offer."

Teen Space features several new multimedia computers, music listening stations, a games area with networked consoles and a much-increased young adult collection of books, graphic novels and magazine.

Director Biblioteca drew special attention to the design of the space. "Our young adults were hands on in giving everything from the furniture to the choice of paint their own personal stamp of approval."

Teen Space will open on July 1. A concert featuring local teen bands will take place at 7 P.M. Patrons of all ages are invited.

For more information visit the library's Web site at http://www.exam plecitylibrary.com or contact John Q. Bibliophile, Young Adult Librarian at (555) 555-5555.

###

INDEX